KW-325-789

TROUBLE WITH THE TAXMAN?

OFFSHORE SURVIVAL

SINK OR SWIM?

THE AUTHORS

Rick Helsby — Partner — based in London, is the national coordinator of the Deloitte Tax Investigations team and has been working in the private sector for over three years. Previously he was a Senior Inspector of Taxes working within London Enquiry Branch of the Inland Revenue for six years.

Jim McMahon — Partner — based in Birmingham, is in charge of the Deloitte's Midlands Region Tax Investigations unit. He too has been with Deloitte for over three years, having previously been a Senior Inspector of Taxes with over four years' experience in Special Office.

Bernard McCarthy — Partner — based in Liverpool, is responsible for the Northern Region Tax Investigations unit. Previously he was a Senior Inspector of Taxes, with three years' experience in Special Office.

With their high level of experience in the field of Inland Revenue investigations, these experts have an unparalleled ability to deal with taxpayers' problems in this area.

CONTENTS

Chapter *Page*

The authors and publishers gratefully acknowledge the
kind permission of the Controller of Her Majesty's
Stationery Office to reproduce the material in
Appendices 1,2,3,5,6 and 9 of this book.

ISBN 0 86349 132 4

© Deloitte Haskins & Sells, UK. August 1988
Photoset by Wordbase Ltd., London
Printed in England by Flexiprint Ltd., Lancing, W. Sussex.

INTRODUCTION

This publication is not intended as a technical textbook for the tax specialist. It is primarily aimed at the non-specialist, who in his business or personal affairs may be considering, or asked to advise on, the use of offshore taxation planning through 'tax havens', although the specialist may find some of the practical comments helpful. The book focuses on a number of key potential problem areas, and seeks to explain issues that may frequently arise and how these are likely to be viewed by the Inland Revenue. It does not pretend to be exhaustive. For instance, it does not cover controlled foreign companies, VAT and custom duties, or inheritance tax.

We have not sought to define the concept of tax haven, except to give here the description used in the recent OECD publication *International Tax Avoidance and Evasion:*

> the 'classical tax haven' may be regarded as a jurisdiction actively making itself available as a tax haven for avoidance of tax which would otherwise be paid in relatively high tax countries. Usually, the aim of the legislation of a classical tax haven is to attract income from activities which are to be carried on outside the territory of the tax haven.

There seems to be a place for the present book in today's climate. Anybody reading the current financial press will appreciate that the Inland Revenue has been developing its techniques and tactics in combating what it sees as objectionable offshore tax planning. Many of the arrangements now under attack were formulated in the early and mid-1970s when the tax planning climate was not as it is today, and when the Inland Revenue's level of knowledge and understanding of the arrangements was limited.

This book therefore aims to cover:

● some of the concepts concerned with residence and domicile and their impact on offshore planning;

● common situations, with particular reference to individuals and family companies, where offshore planning is often contemplated;

● the Inland Revenue's current approach to offshore avoidance and the use of its specialist investigation agencies;

INTRODUCTION

- the practical approaches adopted by the Inland Revenue in investigating arrangements with an offshore aspect;

- the Inland Revenue's information powers and how these are used; and

- the consequences of failed offshore planning.

The Income and Corporation Taxes Act 1988 (ICTA 1988) has, with some exceptions, consolidated the Income and Corporation Taxes Act 1970 (ICTA 1970) and subsequent Finance Acts. References throughout this text are to the new legislation.

This book takes account of the provisions of the Finance Act 1988.

1. TAX RESIDENCE AND DOMICILE

Residence, and to a lesser extent domicile, are fundamental in deciding what UK tax liabilities will arise but, before examining the taxation consequences and ideas behind residence and domicile, it is important to understand that for UK tax purposes:

- 'residence' and 'domicile' are separate and distinct concepts;
- there is a status of 'ordinarily resident' which does not necessarily follow residence;
- the residence tests as applied to an individual, a company and a trust are different; and
- 'domicile' is a concept which, in this context, is generally only applied to an individual.

Different residence tests are applied to individuals, companies and trusts. The tests that apply to individuals and companies are set out below. Trusts are so often used in offshore planning that a separate chapter (Chapter 2) has been included on their residence position and use.

INDIVIDUAL

Chargeability to UK tax

It is a basic principle that UK income tax is charged on any income, whether generated in the UK or elsewhere in the world, that arises to an individual who is resident in the UK. A similar principle applies to capital gains — i.e. worldwide gains are assessed in the UK on a resident individual — with the added proviso that, even where the individual has managed to break the residence link for a particular year, gains are still assessable in the UK where the individual remains *ordinarily resident* in the UK. These basic principles are qualified in a number of respects in certain instances, which are discussed later in this book.

Residence

No statutory test is laid down. The guidelines are those given by the Courts and are summarised in the Inland Revenue's booklet IR 20 (see Appendix 1). But, as that booklet states, each case has to be decided on its own facts.

3

However, in general terms, an individual will be treated as resident in the UK if:

- he has left the UK for the purpose only of *occasional residence* abroad;

- he makes visits to the UK which are both substantial and habitual. 'Substantial' is taken to mean an average of three months or more each year and visits are considered 'habitual' after four consecutive years; from that time he will be regarded as resident in the UK (if it was clear from the outset that such visits were intended, then he may be treated as resident from an earlier period);

- he is physically present in the UK for six months or more in the tax-year, given that six months are equivalent to 183 days and days of arrival and departure are ignored; or

- he makes any visit to the UK, no matter how short, at a time when he has accommodation available for his use unless:

  (a) he works full-time in a trade, profession or vocation which is carried on entirely abroad; or

  (b) he is in full-time employment, all the duties of which, barring incidental ones, are carried out overseas. The 'incidental' test is a qualitative not a quantative one.

Physical presence in the UK is therefore a central issue when considering the residence position of an individual. Although there is nothing laid down in the Taxes Acts on the point, it is generally accepted that an individual who is absent from the UK for a full tax-year will not be resident for UK tax purposes. So the Inland Revenue needs to have evidence of some physical presence in the UK in the year of assessment, no matter how brief, to establish the taxpayer's residence.

However, it is not easy for a UK-resident individual to break his link with the UK if he has continuing business or personal connections there. But, in an era of greater international business and travel, the Court, in the recent case of *Reed v. Clark* [1985] STC 323, seemed to take a view slightly more favourable to the taxpayer.

In July 1988, the Inland Revenue published a Consultative Document, dealing with possible changes to the residence rules for individuals for tax purposes. The stated aim of the Government in the Inland Revenue Press Release announcing the Document was:

> to move in the direction of greater simplicity, certainty and neutrality, and to relate liabilities to UK tax more closely to the degree of an individual's connection with [the UK].

It remains to be seen what legislative changes (if any) will emerge after the consultation period.

Ordinary residence in the UK/Occasional residence abroad

The Courts have attempted to define these two concepts and have viewed them as being the mirror image of or diametrically opposed to each other. Both concepts are important. Following case law, the Inland Revenue interprets the status of ordinary residence as broadly being equivalent to 'habitual residence' and as having an adhesive quality which is more difficult to shake off than simple residence. Occasional residence abroad is something of a temporary nature, with no underlying substantial quality that would break the longer-term link with the UK.

Where, therefore, as we have seen, an individual remains ordinarily resident in the UK, he can still remain liable to capital gains tax even though he was technically non-resident in the particular tax-year in which the sale was carried out. Ordinary residence is also a critical aspect in considering the Inland Revenue's anti-avoidance provisions (see Chapter 3 below).

Occasional residence abroad may be of significance in relation to individuals who are British subjects. Where a British subject has left the UK only for the purposes of occasional residence abroad, then the Taxes Acts can still deem him to be resident in the UK, with all the taxation consequences of that status.

Domicile

Apart from the question of deemed domicile for inheritance tax purposes, or definitions in double taxation agreements, both of which are outside the scope of this book, an individual's domicile is not defined in UK tax law and is determined by general law. In broad terms, a 'domicile' is the place where the individual has his permanent home, although in reality domicile is a much more complex subject. Everyone has a domicile of origin at birth; this may in due course be replaced by a domicile of choice. The domicile of origin depends on the domicile of the person upon whom the individual is legally dependent at the time of the individual's birth.

On reaching maturity, an individual may change his domicile. In order to achieve this it is necessary for him to reside in a country other than that of his original domicile with the intention of staying there and making that country his permanent home.

It was the case that the domicile of women automatically became on marriage that of their husband. This was known as a domicile of dependency. That is no longer the case for marriages after 1973. Where a wife acquired a domicile of dependency on marriage before 1974, it may now be possible for her to prove that she has acquired or reacquired a domicile distinct from that of her husband.

For an individual who is not domiciled in the UK, there are substantial taxation advantages in that overseas income and gains are taxed on a 'remittance' basis rather than an 'arising' basis. It is therefore usually essential for individuals coming to the UK who are not domiciled there to protect their domicile of origin during their time in the UK.

There are occasions where an individual who was domiciled at birth in the UK leaves the country, acquires a new domicile of choice and then comes back to the UK, for example for the education of his children. The Inland Revenue will normally seek to reinstate a UK domicile of origin in such situations.

Domicile can have an important effect as far as non-UK income and capital gains are concerned. If a resident individual is not domiciled in the UK, his non-UK income and gains are not assessed as they arise but only if they are remitted to the UK. This would mean that, if a non-domiciled individual has a Jersey deposit account, the interest which arises is not taxable in the UK provided it is not remitted here. The arrangement and positioning of assets belonging to a non-domiciled individual therefore present opportunities for tax planning. If that individual is about to come to the UK, this has particular importance.

Decisions on an individual's residence and domicile are not made in local tax districts but by a Head Office unit, Claims Branch, in Bootle. In some situations, it may be that an individual is technically resident in more than one country and here the provisions of any double taxation agreement would come into play.

As residence and domicile are of such fundamental importance in tax planning, it is essential that any correspondence with the Inland Revenue on these areas be conducted with an awareness of all the implications. It may well be that professional advice should be sought from the outset.

Fundamental changes to the law governing domicile are currently being considered. If these are implemented, a complete review will be necessary by any non-UK domiciled individual now living in the UK.

COMPANY

A *UK-resident company* is taxable on its worldwide profits including chargeable gains. A *non-resident company* can be liable to UK tax if it is trading in the UK or has income arising in the UK.

Residence

Until the Finance Act 1988, there had never been any general rule laid down by legislation to determine where a company was resident. Now a company will be deemed to be resident in the UK if it is incorporated there unless it was non-resident immediately before 15 March 1988. Moreover, certain of these non-resident companies incorporated in the UK prior to 15 March 1988 will become resident in the UK by 15 March 1993 at the latest.

However, subject to this, the key principle that has emerged from Court decisions over many years is that a company resides where 'the central management and control actually abides'. The 'central management and control' test is an old one but has been endorsed by decisions in later years. The Inland Revenue published a Statement of Practice (6/83) on 27 July 1983 which is reproduced in Appendix 2.

So, to decide whether or not a company incorporated in a tax haven is resident in the UK, it is necessary to locate its place of central management and control. In general terms this test is directed at the highest level of control of a company. As such, the place of central management and control can be distinguished from the place where the main operations of its business are to be found, although obviously the two may coincide.

Case law has also shown that the location of central management and control is a question of fact and has attached importance to the place where the company's board of directors meet. However, the location of board meetings, while important, is not necessarily conclusive. It is significant only in so far as those meetings constitute the medium through which central control and management are exercised. In considering any particular case, the Inland Revenue will usually follow the approach of:

- establishing whether the directors of the company in fact exercise central management and control;

- if so, determining where the directors exercise this control (which is not necessarily where they meet); and

- in any case where the directors apparently do not exercise this control, establishing where and by whom it is exercised.

An illustration of the Inland Revenue's approach would be where a UK-resident individual has set up a company outside the UK which he controls either directly or indirectly. Nominee directors are appointed and all board meetings are held outside the UK. On any review, the Inland Revenue will question the residence of the offshore company. The fact that there was a UK-resident individual who could exercise control over the non-resident directors would almost inevitably lead the Inland Revenue to the conclusion that the company was resident where the controlling shareholder was resident. This would therefore bring the company within the charge to UK corporation tax.

The 'central management and control' test is particularly difficult to apply in a parent/subsidiary relationship where companies operate in different countries. It is normal in this situation for the parent to influence to some extent the actions of the subsidiary. Where this influence is exerted by the parent exercising powers that a sole shareholder has in any general meeting of a subsidiary, e.g. to appoint and dismiss members of the board, or to initiate alterations to its financial structure, the Inland Revenue does not normally seek to argue that the central management and control of the subsidiary is located where the parent company is resident. However, where the parent usurps the function of the board of the subsidiary, or the subsidiary board merely 'rubber stamps' the parent company's decisions without giving any independent thought to them, the Inland Revenue will draw the conclusion that the subsidiary has the same residence for tax purposes as its parent. Its next step might then be to make assessments to UK tax on the subsidiary. These would of course be subject to the normal appeal procedures.

Clearly there will be circumstances where it is difficult to see into which category a subsidiary company falls. In deciding whether the board of the subsidiary company exercises central control, the Inland Revenue will look at the degree of autonomy that the subsidiary directors have in conducting their company's business. One of the main matters to be taken into account is the extent to which the directors of the subsidiaries take decisions on their own authority on investment, marketing and forward planning without reference to the parent.

'Branches or agencies' should also be mentioned briefly. A non-resident company may be liable to UK corporation tax on its income and gains if it has traded in the UK through a branch or agency. This is discussed in Chapter 6 below.

Finally, a non resident company may be liable to income tax in the UK, even where no branch or agency is involved, if it has income arising or trades in the UK. (Double taxation agreements may preclude assessment in many circumstances.)

SUMMARY

This chapter has attempted to show that where at first glance it might seem easy for an individual to leave the UK, or to arrange to set up a company which is not UK-resident, as a way of escaping UK tax liability, in practice the situation is more complex. For example, it is not always easy for an individual who is selling his family business to leave the UK for sufficient time to establish that he is not resident or ordinarily resident before the sale has been carried out. Last-minute residence changes and offshore tax planning are generally destined for failure if scrutinised by the Inland Revenue. Careful and timely planning, with realistic objectives entered into at an early stage, can succeed in appropriate circumstances.

2. SETTLEMENTS OR TRUSTS WITH AN OVERSEAS ELEMENT

WHAT IS A TRUST?

A trust is an independent legal entity, whereby one person (the settlor) gives property to certain persons (the trustees) to hold on behalf of, and for the benefit of, himself or others (the beneficiaries). The basis upon which the trustees may act is normally set out in a deed, which may impose constraints upon how they can use the funds or assets vested in them.

The term 'trust' is not defined in taxation law, which generally makes little distinction between 'trusts' and 'settlements' (and indeed largely refers to 'settlements'), but is founded on general legal concepts. For example, if Mr A gives 25 shares in his company to trustees to hold on behalf of his minor children in equal shares, he will have created a trust. However, Mr A can still retain an element of control over the assets by, for example, being himself appointed as a trustee. The trust may, therefore, be an attractive alternative to an outright gift.

The popularity of trusts in tax planning arises from the fact that a trust can be treated as a separate entity for tax purposes and that its taxation status can be determined independently from that of the settlor. It is therefore possible to create a trust that is not resident in the UK either for income tax or capital gains tax purposes when the settlor of the trust and indeed the beneficiaries are themselves resident. This ability to establish a separate identity outside the UK gives substantial planning opportunities both in the control of the flow of income and in the realisation of capital gains without immediate UK liabilities. As a simple illustration, consider, in the example quoted above, that on the establishment of Mr A's company, 25 shares are transferred to trustees who are not resident in the UK for capital gains tax purposes; the shares are worth £1 each at that time, and 10 years later the company goes to the USM with the settled shares now worth £1 million. On the disposal of those shares by the trustees, no liability to UK capital gains tax will arise, unless capital payments are received by beneficiaries resident in the UK. The gains can therefore be retained in the trust until such time as capital is required, and indeed if the beneficiaries have become non-resident at the date at which the capital passes to them, no liability to UK capital gains will arise at all.

10

WHAT IS AN OVERSEAS TRUST?

There are two tests. The first concerns the residence of the trustees. The second concerns the administration of the trust.

For income tax purposes, the trust will not be UK-resident if all the trustees are resident outside the UK and the administration of the trust is carried on outside this country.

For capital gains tax the test is somewhat less demanding. Here only the majority of the trustees have to be resident outside the UK, but once again the administration must be carried on outside the UK.

With capital gains now to be taxed at income rates, following the Finance Act 1988, any significant gains that have arisen post-1982, and that are now realised by individuals, will be taxed at 40%. Capital gains tax planning and the placing of assets into the correct structure before their value increases will have a growing importance. So the use of non-resident trusts is a particularly topical issue.

As it is not difficult to arrange to have trustees resident outside the UK and to have the trust administered outside this country, it is fairly straightforward to establish a non-resident trust. In addition, a trust created by a non-domiciled individual who is neither resident nor ordinarily resident in the UK will be treated as not resident in the UK even if it is administered in the UK, as long as the majority of the trustees are non-resident.

HOW IN PRACTICE IS CONTROL EXERCISED OVER TRUST ASSETS?

If a UK trust is established, then the settlor, Mr A in the example above, can himself be a trustee or use suitable professional advisors. The trust will also be under the jurisdiction of the UK Courts, assuming it is written under English, Scottish or Northern Irish law, and so Mr A's position is well protected. Taxpayers do have concerns, however, where trusts are established outside the UK with non-resident trustees not known to them.

There are a number of ways in which our Mr A can be reassured in such circumstances. The first is to choose a location and trustees where the laws of that jurisdiction and the standing of the trustees are such that problems are not likely to arise.

Additionally, Mr A can send to the trustees what is known as a *letter of wishes*. This, in practical terms, is a statement of how he would like the trustees to deal with the assets. Although the trustees are not legally bound to take cognizance of this letter, in most instances they will pay attention to it in making decisions. A further level of comfort would be the use of a *protector* and the writing of the trust deed in such a way that the trustees are not empowered to undertake certain actions unless given authority by the protector. Typically a protector would be a trusted friend or professional advisor, preferably resident outside the UK. His role would be to block any acts by the trustees which are contrary to the original aims of the settlement.

The above general outline applies to countries with jurisdictions which have a legal system based on or similar to English law. There are a number of European countries where similar concepts are dealt with by different legal entities. In Liechtenstein, for example, there is a trust concept (the *Treuunternehmen* (trust enterprise)), not dissimilar to the trust under English law, whereas that country also has other entities, e.g. *Anstalts* (establishments) and *Stiftungs* (foundations), with no UK equivalent. Most of the points made in relation to planning will equally apply to such entities and the Inland Revenue will take just as detailed an interest in their use.

DISCRETIONARY TRUSTS

In the example of Mr A quoted above, the position could be changed if the trustees were given the discretion as to what amounts to pay to the beneficiaries, and indeed to decide which beneficiaries in the class of beneficiary mentioned in the trust deed should benefit. This is the essence of a discretionary trust, which has a great deal more flexibility than a trust where the shares of individuals who are entitled to both the income and capital have already been fixed. A discretionary settlement, however, might be useful where income has arisen outside the UK and no payments have been made to UK beneficiaries. Income can in such circumstances accumulate outside the UK free of UK tax until such time as payments are made to UK beneficiaries. So, our Mr A, instead of settling 25 shares on a non-resident fixed interest settlement, would

- transfer £100,000 to a non-resident discretionary settlement, from which he and his spouse are excluded from all benefit; and
- the beneficiaries would be Mr A's three children.

The trust would then invest £100,000 outside the UK, and the income that accumulates would be free from UK tax until any payments are made to the beneficiaries. If any of the beneficiaries are non-UK resident, payments of income to them will be free of UK tax.

3. UK ANTI-AVOIDANCE LEGISLATION

BRIEF OUTLINE

As suggested in Chapter 1 above, the UK Inland Revenue aims, as a general principle, to assess profits from UK residents from whatever source these profits derive, and from non-UK residents in respect of profits derived from UK activities.

The legislation to which this chapter refers is that devised to counter situations where UK residents seek to escape the UK tax net by putting assets or income outside the scope of UK tax, or by limiting their UK taxable profits through pricing arrangements with non-UK residents.

The legislation has developed over a considerable period – that now contained in s.739 ICTA 1988 was first enacted in the Finance Act 1936.

This chapter summarises the main provisions as far as they have an impact on offshore arrangements.

SECTION 739 ICTA 1988 – TRANSFER OF ASSETS ABROAD

Section 739 ICTA 1988 itself explains that it has been devised:

> for the purpose of preventing the avoiding by individuals ordinarily resident in the United Kingdom of liability to income tax by means of transfers of assets by virtue or in consequence where, either alone or in conjunction with associated operations, income becomes payable to persons resident or domiciled out of the UK.

This principle, not entirely simple in itself, has led to the very complex provisions contained at ss.739, 741-743 and 746 ICTA 1988 (and information powers in s.745 ICTA 1988 discussed in Chapter 4 below), which have been considered by the Courts in a number of tax cases. While an entire volume could be written about this legislation, only the main aspects will be considered here.

The thinking behind s.739 is relatively simple. As income arising outside the UK of an individual who is neither resident nor domiciled within the UK does not fall within the charge to UK tax, an individual resident in the UK could (but for the UK anti-avoidance provisions) avoid UK income tax by transferring income-producing assets to, for example, the trustees of a foreign settlement made by him and of which he was or could be a beneficiary.

The provisions of s.739(1)–(4) were therefore designed to counter that situation. They apply where:

Section 739(2)

- there is a transfer of assets

- income becomes payable to non-resident or non-domiciled persons (including companies), and

- an individual ordinarily resident in UK has *power to enjoy any income* of the non-resident or non-domiciled person, and

- that income would otherwise be chargeable to UK tax.

Section 739(3)

- there is a transfer of assets

- income becomes payable to non-resident or non-domiciled persons (including companies), and

- an individual ordinarily resident in the UK receives a *capital sum before or after the transfer* in connection with that transfer or any associated operation.

In such cases the income of the non-resident or non domiciled person is deemed to be the income of the individual having the power to enjoy the income or receiving the capital sum for all UK tax purposes.

This raises the issue of the meaning of 'power to enjoy' (s.739(2)) and 'capital sum' (s.739(3)–(5)). These expressions are very widely drawn and mean that an individual can be deemed to have *power to enjoy* overseas income if, for example:

- the transfer increases the value of any assets held by him for his benefit; or

- he receives or is entitled to receive any benefit provided out of the income; or

- he has the ability to control the application of the income; or

- with the exercise of powers, by him or any other party, he can become entitled to the beneficial enjoyment of the income.

The term '*capital sum*' will cover:

- amounts paid or payable by way of loan or repayment of loan, or

- any amounts paid otherwise than as income, where the payment is not for full consideration in money or money's worth.

The scope of s.739 (or s.478 ICTA 1970, as it then was) was significantly reduced as a consequence of the House of Lords' decision in the 1979 case of *Vestey v. CIR* [1980] STC 10, and the legislation was subsequently amended by the provisions of s.45 Finance Act 1981 (now largely contained in s.740 ICTA 1988).

Prior to the *Vestey* decision, it was thought that any beneficiary of such an arrangement could be assessed on *all* the income arising outside the UK. The *Vestey* decision meant that where the transferor and his spouse were totally excluded from the power to enjoy or to receive a capital sum, there could be no s.739 charge on them or on any other beneficiaries. In that situation, a charge would now arise on other beneficiaries under s.740 ICTA 1988. However such a charge will only apply where sums are appointed or attributed to UK-resident individuals. In other words, 'power to enjoy', etc., is no longer sufficient to trigger a charge in relation to non-transferors (i.e. the beneficiaries); cash or benefits must be received by individual beneficiaries who are resident in the UK. This raises the possibility that sums can be accumulated within the non-resident trust free of tax, with liability only arising when they are distributed to UK-resident individuals.

In addition to addressing the position of non-transferors, the Finance Act 1981 extended the already wide definition of 'power to enjoy' in relation to transferors. This now includes situations where, although there is no legal right to income, the substance of the transaction is such that benefits accrue to the transferor.

There are some other important exemptions relating to s.739, broadly as follows:

- The provisions relate, as can be seen, to individuals and not to companies. This does not mean, however, that if a family company is involved in offshore avoidance, the Inland Revenue is necessarily precluded from pursuing the individual directors or shareholders under s.739. This is covered in Chapter 5 below.

- Also, it should be noted that the provisions relate to individuals 'ordinarily resident' in the UK. Section 739 is aimed at individuals with a permanent presence in the UK, and not at individuals who are simply 'resident' without being ordinarily resident. This does not mean, however, that any transfer which takes place when an individual is not ordinarily resident escapes the section should the individual subsequently become

16

ordinarily resident – a point often overlooked.

● Where an individual can demonstrate to the satisfaction of the Board of Inland Revenue that avoiding a liability to tax was not the reason why the transfer (or other operations) were effected, or that the transfer was a *bona fide* commercial transaction and not designed for the purposes of avoiding a liability to tax, he will be exempted. The problem is that, because there is no advance clearance procedure, an individual who thinks he falls within one of those categories will have to go ahead in the anticipation that he will be able to satisfy the Board (with appeal rights to the Special Commissioners) that this exemption is appropriate.

● Where an individual is *domiciled* outside the UK, he is exempted in respect of any deemed income if, by virtue of his domicile, he would not have been taxed on it if it had been his actual income, e.g. where the remittance basis would be applicable and the sum was not remitted. (Where sums are subsequently remitted, they will probably be charged within the tax-year of remittance.)

In practice, the provisions of s.739 are probably the least understood and most litigated of all anti-avoidance provisions. Any attempt at offshore planning for an individual should include an appraisal of the potential exposure under these provisions.

SECTION 765 ICTA 1988 – MIGRATION OF COMPANIES

The factors determining the residence of companies have been considered already in Chapter 1 above. The position of a branch or agency of a non-resident company will be discussed separately.

The Finance Act 1988 changes the legislation designed to counter tax avoidance by company migration (s.765).

Where a company is incorporated in the UK, it will not now cease to be resident if its central management and control is transferred outside the UK. If a company incorporated outside the UK ceases to be resident in the UK, it must obtain Inland Revenue approval before doing so, and on ceasing to be resident in the UK it will be deemed to have sold and reacquired all its assets for capital gains purposes. A similar deemed disposal of assets will apply where any company resident in the UK ceases to be liable to UK corporation tax by becoming exempt under the terms of a double taxation agreement. If the trade or business is transferred to a non-resident company, the existing rules for determining tax liabilities on the transfer, including corporation tax on capital gains, will continue to apply to a UK-resident company.

There are a few special circumstances under which Treasury Consent is still required under s.765, and specialist advice should always be taken where it is proposed to transfer a company or its assets outside the UK, or to transfer or issue shares or debentures of a non-resident company that is under the control of a UK-resident company.

SECTION 770 ICTA 1988 – TRANSFER PRICING

Because there is no law requiring a person to maximise profits from a transaction, it is possible that the UK Inland Revenue could lose tax by goods or services being supplied at under or over value to or from companies outside the UK. For this reason s.770 ICTA 1988 enacts specific provisions where sales or services between associated persons are at prices other than might have been expected had the transaction been to independent people dealing at arm's length. It is worth noting that many overseas tax authorities have similar legislation.

Section 770 ICTA 1988 applies where:

- the buyer is a body of persons (which includes a partnership) over whom the seller has control;
- the seller is a body of persons over whom the buyer has control; or
- both the seller and the buyer are bodies of persons over whom some other person has control,

and enables an arm's-length value to be attributed to the sales or services provided.

In this way the Inland Revenue is able to counteract transactions between UK and overseas companies, which would otherwise lead to a UK tax liability being mitigated and replaced with a liability in an overseas régime with a lower rate of tax.

The Inland Revenue's guidance notes on s.485 ICTA 1970 (the predecessor of s.770) and transfer pricing were issued on 26 January 1981, and are shown in Appendix 3. The Inland Revenue polices the legislation through a specialist Head Office section, and formal information powers exist which are discussed in Chapter 4 below.

Section 775 – income from personal activities

Section 775 ICTA 1988 aims to counteract avoidance exercises whereby the earning capacity of an individual is disposed of for a capital sum, and his income is not therefore taxed as income. It charges such capital sums to income tax (under Schedule D Case VI), where tax avoidance was the purpose of the exercise. It is sometimes thought that it only applies to the entertainment and sports industries, but it extends to any activity of a professional nature, whether carried on in a self-employed or an employed capacity. The section, therefore, should not be overlooked in any situation where the income or capital is derived outside the UK.

Section 776 – Artificial transactions in land

As for s.739 ICTA 1988, the purposes of this section are clearly stated:

> to prevent the avoidance of tax by persons concerned with
> land or the development of land.

The section itself makes it clear that transactions that are not artificial and transactions not directly in land may be caught. Having said that, the provisions are particularly important where there is an attempt to move value deriving from land offshore.

The effect is to tax as income (under Schedule D Case VI) all profits obtained, whether directly or not, from land or interests in land, and the section can apply to all persons whether resident or not in the UK provided that all or any part of the land is in the UK.

Section 776 can apply where there is a disposal:

- by the person who acquired the land or who held or developed it;
- by a person 'connected' with him – i.e., broadly, relatives or companies under common control, or connected settlors or trustees of a trust;
- by a person party to a scheme or arrangement concerning the land; or
- by a person who has had the opportunity of making a gain and transmits this opportunity.

A simple example would be where Company A owns land worth £100,000, which, if planning permission is granted, would be worth £1 million. It sells the land, before planning permission is granted, at market value to an offshore 'connected' company, Company B. Planning permission is then granted and the land is sold by non-resident Company B for £1 million. Profits on the overall transaction of £900,000 could be assessed on Company A under s.776.

Section 777

So far as any offshore dimension is concerned, s.777 is relevant in relation to both ss.775 and 776. It aims to counteract attempts to avoid those provisions by allowing the Inland Revenue to follow through transactions by companies, trusts, etc. and enables tax to be recovered from anybody in receipt of the proceeds.

Section 777 applies where it appears that any property or right is transferred, or that the value of any property or right is enhanced or diminished. Of particular note is s.777(9), which enables the Board of Inland Revenue to order that tax be deducted at source (under s.349(1) ICTA 1988) by the payer of any consideration (the purchaser), where the person entitled to the proceeds of the sale (the vendor) is *not resident* in the UK. A purchaser who is subject to such deduction is entitled for his part to recover the tax that has been paid over to the Inland Revenue from the person entitled to the proceeds of sale. Taking the example of a property deal that may fall within s.776, if the Inland Revenue approach the potential purchaser under s.777(9), this could lead to the parties to the transaction reconsidering the basis of the deal itself.

It should also be noted that s.777(13) defines 'the capital amount' as any amount, in money or money's worth, that otherwise does not fall to be included as income in the Taxes Acts.

CLEARANCE PROCEDURES

A clearance procedure is available under s.776(11) but, as it is difficult to obtain Inland Revenue clearance, careful consideration should be given as to whether to make an application.

SETTLEMENT LEGISLATION

This book does not intend to look in detail at the complicated specific anti-avoidance legislation regarding settlements contained in the Taxes Acts. This is because it would be unusual for the Inland Revenue to use that legislation in its initial approach to offshore avoidance relating to overseas trusts. The provisions of s.739 ICTA 1988, in any case, are very widely drawn, and will probably cover all but the following circumstances:

- where the *bona fide* commercial exemption under s.739 would be applicable; or

- where payments are made from a settlement, from which the settlor is excluded, to his minor children – subject to the possibility that the children would be caught under the provisions of s.740 ICTA 1988.

CAPITAL GAINS TAX

A potentially straightforward way of avoiding UK capital gains tax would be to have the chargeable assets held by a non-resident company. The gains on disposal would not be assessable under s.739 because they would not represent income. However, there is anti-avoidance legislation that deals with such gains. Where a non-resident company is a close company (i.e. broadly controlled by directors or up to five shareholders), and there are UK-resident shareholders, gains arising in the company are apportioned to the UK-resident shareholders. For example, Mr A and Mr B each own 50% of the shares in Jersey Company C and C realises a capital gain of £100,000 in 1988/89; such gains, i.e. £50,000 each, would be apportioned to the UK-resident shareholders A and B under the provisions of s.15 CGTA 1979 and assessed for the same tax-year.

TRUSTS

The residence position of trusts was covered in Chapter 2 above. If a trust is not resident in the UK for capital gains tax purposes, gains arising on the trustees are not liable in the UK unless capital payments are received by UK-resident beneficiaries of the trust. Where capital payments are received by the UK beneficiaries, the gains arising to the trustees can be apportioned to the beneficiaries. 'Capital payments' are defined broadly in the same way as those for the purposes of s.739 ICTA 1988: see above. The gains will be taxed in the tax-year in which the capital payments are received. It is thus possible to defer capital gains. For example where a non-resident trust has capital gains of £100,000 in 1988/89 and in 1992/93 capital payments of £50,000 each are made to the two UK beneficiaries, UK capital gains tax will not arise until 1992/93, when gains will be assessed on the UK individuals, subject to their annual exemptions. If, in this example, the gains had been £150,000, the only gains assessed in 1992/93 would be £50,000 in each case, as before; i.e. the gains would be assessed up to the amount of the capital payments received. However, the excess gains of £50,000 not matched with capital payments would be matched with capital payments made in later years up to the amount of that excess, and assessments made accordingly.

Some other aspects of non-resident trusts are mentioned in Chapter 5 below.

4. SOURCES OF INFORMATION

In order to attack arrangements that may have UK tax consequences, the Inland Revenue will need to establish all available facts in order to be able to show the appellate Commissioners, who act as independent arbiters on tax appeals, or in the unusual event that criminal proceedings are contemplated, the Courts, that there is, at the least, a case to answer.

Any contemplated avoidance arrangement should therefore begin with the question: if the Inland Revenue were aware of all the facts, would the arrangements succeed? If the answer is 'no', or a qualified 'no', then it would be unsafe to carry through the arrangements.

Arrangements are often contemplated or activated in the belief that the Inland Revenue can never become aware of all the facts. It is important to understand, therefore, the very considerable powers that the Inland Revenue does have, and is using with increasing effect, to obtain the facts.

FOREIGN REVENUE AUTHORITIES

Most double taxation agreements include provisions for the exchange of information between the UK and revenues authorities overseas. An example is the agreement with Jersey which provides that.

> the taxation authorities of the United Kingdom and Jersey shall exchange such information . . . as is necessary . . . for the prevention of fraud or the administration of the statutory provisions against legal avoidance in relation to the taxes which are the subject of this arrangement.

The readiness with which such provisions are used or contemplated depends to a degree on how individuals or respective departments have sought to develop the formal application of the provisions. For example, an overseas authority may do no more than confirm or deny matters put to it by the Inland Revenue, or it may go further and seek actively to assist the UK authorities by, for example, carrying out research to establish additional facts.

Formal requests for information are channelled through Inland Revenue Special Offices, which have been instrumental over the last few years in developing both the informal and formal links with foreign revenue authorities. People involved in international operations should be aware of the increasing exchange of information, and cannot therefore assume that different sets of facts can be placed before different revenue authorities without risk.

PUBLIC RECORD INFORMATION

The Inland Revenue can obtain significant amounts of information through the public records that exist in tax haven countries.

In Appendix 4 below we have summarised information that would be available in some tax havens.

CUSTOMS & EXCISE

Section 127 Finance Act 1972 provides for Customs & Excise and the Inland Revenue to exchange information. This power is widely used. Until recently, formal requests had to be channelled through Enquiry Branch, but now it has been announced that the Inland Revenue and Customs & Excise can exchange information at local-office level.

It is also possible for Customs & Excise to conduct a control visit with a view to establishing certain facts that the Inland Revenue might also find useful. The Inland Revenue's powers of entering premises are far more limited and do not extend beyond PAYE audit vists, where only payroll, etc., records need to be produced, save for a s.20C TMA 1970 search operation as described in Chapter 6 below. But a Customs & Excise visit could, for example, be used to obtain first-hand evidence of the UK end of offshore invoicing arrangements, or indeed could trigger an Inland Revenue investigation as a result of Customs & Excise researches on unrelated matters, which by chance might have uncovered such arrangements.

DISTRICT VALUERS

District Valuers can provide useful information to Inland Revenue investigation sections, in that they obtain details of all property transactions. Where these involve non-resident vendors or purchasers and a substantial consideration, these may be channelled to Special Office. The opportunity may then be taken to raise enquiries with solicitors and estate agents on the detailed background to the particular transaction. Thus, for example, a wealthy non-domiciled individual settling in the UK and buying a property through an offshore company may well attract Special Office attention.

OTHER SOURCES

There is nothing to prevent the Inland Revenue from seeking information from numerous other official or unofficial sources, albeit that, for its part, it cannot reveal confidential information. For example, the UK immigration authorities could be approached for information, because an applicant for naturalisation will supply the authorities with information as to his background, assets and business interests. The police or the divorce registry could be approached for information if it was thought this could be helpful.

Newspapers and other published information provide useful material. There are other published sources such as those concerning movement of shipping which can assist in determining the residence position of individuals.

INFORMERS

Finally, it must not be overlooked in considering informal sources of information that often the most valuable information comes from informers. While they may frequently be motivated by malice or spite, they often produce firm evidence, and the Inland Revenue, in particular Special Office, will seek to exploit such sources to the maximum.

FORMAL INFORMATION POWERS

Precept notices

Precept notices (s.51 TMA 1970), issued by the appellate Commissioners, are addressed to the taxpayer himself, requiring particulars and/or books, records, etc. Precepts, however, can only be obtained if an assessment to tax has been made and is subject to an appeal. The inspector must then show the Commissioners that the information for which he is requesting a precept is relevant for the purpose of determining the appeal. The taxpayer for his part can attend the appeal hearing and argue his case.

Section 20(1) notices

An inspector also has formidable powers under s.20(1) TMA 1970. Where an inspector believes, and can show a Commissioner, that he requires information that may be relevant to a person's tax affairs, he can serve a notice on that person for information which he has or would be able to obtain, without any requirement for an assessment or an appeal to have been made. Unlike an appeal hearing for precepts, the taxpayer is not entitled to be present at the s.20 notice application. However an informal request for the information must have been provided to the taxpayer before a formal notice is sought. Section 20(1) notices could, for example, request credit card statements, which could be used by the inspector to show that an individual must have been resident in the UK, contrary to the taxpayer's own assertions as to the dates on which he was in the country.

Section 20(3) notices

It is also possible for the Inland Revenue to make an *ex parte* application to obtain information formally from third parties under a s.20(3) notice, although, again, an informal request must initially have been made to the third party for the information.

For example, where an individual is unable or unwilling to supply credit card information himself, the Inland Revenue could turn direct to the credit card company for the information.

The Finance Act 1988 introduces a very significant extension of the s.20(3) powers. Normally notices issued under s.20(3) must name the individual in respect of whom information is sought. In future, and with the Board's authority, an inspector can request a Special Commissioner to order a third party to supply information about a taxpayer or a class of taxpayer whose identity is unknown to the Inland Revenue. The inspector must satisfy the Commissioner that serious tax loss may be involved through the individual(s) not properly complying with provisions of the Taxes Acts, and that the information is not readily available from another source. The recipient of the notice will be entitled to challenge it if its provisions appear unduly onerous. But the new powers will enable the Inland Revenue to request information from, for example, sponsors of tax avoidance arrangements, where large amounts of tax may be involved.

It remains to be seen how, in practice, these powers will be used, but potentially they could prove one of the Inland Revenue's more devastating weapons in their investigations of offshore planning and avoidance.

Failure to comply with s.20 information notices will trigger the penalty provisions of s.98 TMA 1970, i.e. £50 for the initial failure, and thereafter a maximum of £10 per day.

Section 745 notices

Section 745 ICTA 1988 notices are particularly relevant to offshore arrangements. Each notice will be different, depending on the individual facts of the case. What might be a typical notice is given in Appendix 5 for reference. As this example shows, the information requirements can be very wide-ranging.

The Board may require, by notice under s.745, any person (not only the taxpayer) to furnish it with such particulars as the Board think necessary for the purposes of s.739, referred to in Chapter 3. Those particulars are specified as including:

● transactions with respect to which the individual was acting on behalf of others;

● transactions which in the opinion of the Board it is proper that it should investigate for the purposes of s.739, notwithstanding that in the opinion of the person to whom notice is given, no liability to tax arises under s.739; and

● whether the person to whom the notice is given has taken or is taking any, and if so what, part in any, and if so what, transactions of a description specified in the notice.

In other words, the notice is all-embracing, and it is immaterial that the person to whom it is directed thinks that there is no tax consequence.

There are some *exceptions*. In particular, a solicitor is not deemed to have taken part in a transaction where all he has done is given professional advice to a client in connection with that transaction. All he need do in such circumstances is to state that he is acting on behalf of the client and give the name and address of the client. Where he has acted in respect of the transfer of an asset by a resident individual to a non-resident company, he need only detail the name and address of the transferor and transferee. Again, where, in respect of non-resident companies, he has been involved in the formation or management of the company, he need only supply the name and address of the company. Finally, where a solicitor does work in connection with the creation or execution of trusts, and income becomes payable to a non-resident or non-domiciled person, the solicitor needs only to provide the names and addresses of the settlor and of the non-resident or non-domiciled person.

It should also be noted that a bank is not obliged to furnish any particulars of ordinary banking transactions between the bank and the customer carried out in the ordinary course of banking business, unless the bank's actions were on behalf of a customer in connection with the formation or management of a company not resident in the UK or in connection with the formation or management of settlements. In such cases, the same provisions as for solicitors described above apply.

Section 745 notices can be and are used in obtaining information from accountants and other professional advisors. Such notices are an extremely valuable and effective means of collecting information for the Inland Revenue, in relation to offshore arrangements.

NOMINEE SHAREHOLDERS AND NON-RESIDENT COMPANIES AND TRUSTS

Section 26 TMA 1970 can enable a nominee shareholder in a non-resident company to be asked by the Board to provide the names and addresses of the beneficial owners of the shares. Of more practical significance, where an individual or company holds shares in a non-resident company, or has an interest in settled property where the trust itself is not resident, the Board can require these persons, under s.27 TMA 1970, to give particulars to determine whether the company or trust falls within the non-resident sections of the Capital Gains Tax Act 1979 and to provide details of any gains which have accrued.

Although this book does not cover inheritance tax, the Inland Revenue frequently becomes aware of the existence of a non-resident trust by reason of a reporting requirement contained in s. 218 IHTA 1984. Under this section, professional advisors (other than barristers) who are concerned with the making of an *inter vivos* settlement, and who know or have reason to believe that the settlor was UK-domiciled and that the trustees are or will be non-UK-resident, must, within three months of the making of the settlement, send details of the settlor's and trustees' names and addresses to the Inland Revenue.

SECTION 778 ICTA 1988

The Inland Revenue is empowered to require such information as it considers necessary for the purposes of s.776. As with s.745 notices, these will differ according to the precise facts and circumstances of the particular case. By way of illustration, what might be a typical notice in a hypothetical case is given in Appendix 6. In particular, the Inland Revenue can ask for details of:

- transactions and arrangements where a person acted on behalf of others;

- transactions and arrangements which, in the Inland Revenue's opinion, should be properly investigated even though the person on whom the notice is served may consider that s.776 does not apply; and

- confirmation as to whether the person to whom the notice is given has taken part in such transactions or arrangements as are described in the notice.

As with s.745, there is an exclusion from this information power for a solicitor, to the extent that he has given professional advice to a client in connection with the transaction. A solicitor acting for a client cannot be compelled to do more than state that he was acting on behalf of the client in a transaction and give the name and address of the client.

SECTION 772 ICTA 1988

As regards transfer-pricing, there are wide-ranging information powers whereby the Inland Revenue can require details of transactions to which it believes provisions of s.770 apply. Such powers require that books, records, etc., be produced, relating to the transaction, from a UK parent company, where the transaction is between that UK company and a non-resident member of its group.

The Inland Revenue also has the power to enter premises to inspect documentation, where it believes that transactions to which s.770 might apply are involved.

5. COMMON SITUATIONS

This chapter considers certain fairly standard problems that can arise, particularly in relation to family companies, where an attempt has been made to shelter profits offshore. It should be stressed that not all arrangements involving UK family companies trading with tax haven associates are destined to fail if investigated by the Inland Revenue. As with the other arrangements that are discussed in this chapter, it may well be that, with proper planning, realistic objectives and sound implementation, the arrangements can be effective for tax purposes.

PROFIT-SHELTERING BY FAMILY COMPANIES

The shareholder/directors of successful family companies often seek advice on minimising their own or their companies' tax bills. Offshore arrangements are sometimes established where the form of those arrangements does not reflect their true substance. Naturally this will lead to problems with the Inland Revenue. Typically, the form of the arrangements will involve:

- establishment of an offshore entity;
- arrangements for the shareholders/directors to have effective control of that company in a covert way; and
- transactions between the UK and the offshore concern, designed to lodge part of the profits in the offshore concern where no or low tax will be paid.

So how do the arrangements described above work? The shares in an offshore company may be registered in the name of professional nominees, living in a tax haven, who will be paid perhaps £100 per year for allowing their names to be used and for signing documents, etc., when required. Generally, the nominees will have signed blank and undated share-transfer forms which will be held by the UK beneficial owners. Sometimes the beneficial owners will also hold simple declarations, also signed by the nominees, that they hold the shares as bare trustees/nominees for the (named) beneficial owner.

A more sophisticated version of the above is the use of what are commonly known as 'black hole' or 'limbo' trusts. Here, the shares in an offshore company are held in trust by tax haven resident trustees. The trust will be a discretionary trust and the settlor will usually be a 'dummy', often a friend or relative of one of the UK shareholders/directors, who is resident abroad and who provides the

30

original nominal sum to set up the trust. The settlor will usually have provided a 'letter of wishes' to the trustees, telling them that the trust was intended to be for the benefit of the UK shareholders/directors, who should be consulted on all matters relating to the trust. In addition, a protector may have been appointed, who will be a friend or trusted advisor to the shareholder/directors and will live outside the UK. The trustees will be required to consult the protector before exercising certain of their powers under the trust deed.

The objective of such an arrangement is to allow the shareholders/directors to deny ownership of the shares of the offshore company and to be able to state that they are neither settlors nor beneficiaries of any foreign settlement. At the same time, the letter of wishes and protector ensure that the trustees exercise their discretion in accordance with the wishes of the shareholder/directors so that, at the appropriate time, they or their children, perhaps after leaving the UK, can be appointed beneficiaries of the trust and can receive the accumulated profits of the offshore company.

Suppose therefore that a 'limbo trust' controlled offshore company has been set up as described above. How would some of the UK profits be transferred to it? Typical mechanisms are as follows:

- selling products to the offshore company for onward sale to the ultimate customers. The pricing will be so structured as to leave a substantial part of the profit offshore;

- arranging for the offshore company to purchase materials, etc., and sell these on at a higher price to the UK company;

- the making of charges by the offshore company to the UK company for the apparent provision of services. These may be inflated charges for real services such as leasing of equipment or factoring of debts, or may, in some instances, be wholly fictitious, with no service provided; and

- the purchase by the offshore company of plant or machinery, with subsequent resale to the UK company at a significant mark-up on the original cost.

The profits made by the offshore company will be liable to tax at the lower tax haven rate. However it is quite frequently the case that such profits escape taxation entirely. This is achieved, for example, by incorporating an offshore company in the Isle of Man or in Jersey but appointing a majority of directors who are resident in Sark. The company then pays a flat non-resident fee of a few hundred pounds per annum to its territory of registration and pays no tax at all on its profits – the so called 'Sark Lark'.

In many instances these arrangements have, in practice, succeeded because the Inland Revenue has not discovered what was happening and has not therefore investigated or challenged. However in recent times, certainly the last five or six years, the Inland Revenue has become increasingly adept at uncovering, investigating and defeating such schemes, and the Special Offices have been particularly successful in this area. It is worthy of note, however, that Enquiry Branch are now also becoming particularly active. The role and function of these and other specialist investigation agencies are discussed in Chapter 6 below.

Once the facts have been exposed, there are a number of routes by which the Inland Revenue can attack the arrangements; some of these are dealt with below.

SHAM

A typical example of a 'sham' would be a UK manufacturing and sales company where sales are routed through an offshore company, but where all the substantive operations of manufacture, pricing, invoicing and management decisions are taken in the UK and the offshore 'operation' has no staff or establishment and provides no services either to the UK company or to the eventual customers. In such circumstances, the Inland Revenue could argue that the trading profits are all assessable on the UK company, and could seek interest and penalties from the UK company. It may also possibly contend that the offshore funds represent loans or advances to the directors, thus giving rise to a further charge to tax, interest and penalties on the funds 'loaned'.

RESIDENCE STATUS

It may be that there is substance to the operations of the offshore company, but that the effective management and control rests in the UK, with the offshore company 'rubber stamping' decisions made in the UK. This is usually the case with 'Sark Lark' companies. In such circumstances, the Inland Revenue could maintain that the offshore company is resident in the UK, but has failed to disclose its liability to UK tax. Accordingly the Inland Revenue could seek interest and penalties on this non-disclosure. This could, of course, create difficulties for the Inland Revenue in enforcing payment of the tax liability, where the debt is outside the UK jurisdiction.

BRANCH OR AGENCY

Such enforcement difficulties could be overcome if the Inland Revenue could show that the offshore company was trading through the branch or agency of the UK company, or through its UK directors. An assessment could then be raised on the UK company or its directors as agent for the offshore company, and enforcement of the tax, interest and penalties obtained through the provisions of ss.78 and 83 TMA 1970, which are described in Chapter 6 below.

TRANSFER PRICING

Where there is a real commercial substance to the arrangements, the Inland Revenue could make use of the transfer-pricing legislation described in Chapter 3. The provisions of s.770 ICTA 1988 will allow an adjustment to be made to the cross-border pricing to produce a full commercial profit in the UK. An adjustment under this section does not normally attract interest and penalties.

TRANSFER OF ASSETS

It should be borne in mind that, in relation to any ordinarily resident individual (in this case this would normally be the shareholder/director), the Inland Revenue could employ the provisions of s.739 ICTA 1988, the effect of which would be that the profits of the offshore company could be assessed to income tax on the individual concerned. This complex legislation has been considered in Chapter 3 above. Where an offshore trust arrangement is involved, the Inland Revenue may occasionally be precluded from applying s.739. If so, it could consider the possibility of raising assessments under the settlement legislation.

This particular scenario has been considered at some length because it is so frequently met. Certain other aspects of flawed offshore planning are briefly considered below.

REMITTANCES TO NON-DOMICILED INDIVIDUALS

The UK is widely regarded as being a tax haven for individuals who are not domiciled there. As was pointed out in Chapter 1 above, where such individuals have income or gains that arise outside the UK, the income or gains are not taxable provided they are not remitted to the UK.

Problems may arise where non-domiciled individuals come to the UK without previously having taken advice on the proper arrangement of their finances outside the UK. Very briefly, all income and capital that arises outside the UK should be separated and accumulated in different bank accounts. Where such accounts are mixed, all remittances to the UK are treated as coming first out of income and then capital. Where only identifiable capital is remitted, there should not be a UK income tax problem, but the possibility of a UK capital gains tax charge arising should not be overlooked.

Even where proper advice has been taken, non-domiciled individuals frequently find that capital is insufficient to meet their requirements and make income remittances which should be shown on tax returns, and which the Inland Revenue discovers, on close examination of the individual's affairs, to have been omitted:

Equally, attempts made to provide income through alternative routes, for example through loan arrangements, can be attacked. Typically such situations will arise where, in the early stages, income or capital is needed in the UK to purchase accommodation or set up businesses before sufficient UK income is generated to meet such commitments. In practice, therefore, although advice may be obtained at an early stage which sets out in detail the theoretical structure necessary to avoid UK tax, such arrangements are not adhered to and the advisor is often unaware of this. When the Inland Revenue examines such cases in detail, it may well find that there have been 'constructive remittances' to the UK. 'Constructive remittances' can include applications outside the UK, in satisfaction of any debt of money in the UK, of income arising outside the UK.

Where such sums have not been shown on the appropriate income tax return, the Inland Revenue may take the view that interest and penalties should also be recovered from the taxpayer, as well as the tax liability itself. If an in-depth examination is undertaken by the Inland Revenue, this will mean a detailed review of all bank and credit card accounts, both inside and outside the UK, in order to establish income and capital flows.

LAND TRANSACTIONS

One of the most frequent uses of offshore companies is to shelter profits from property transactions. This is probably a reflection of the
fact that successful property deals are perhaps the most common
way in which large profits are generated by a single transaction or a
series of transactions over a short time. Consequently, where such a
profit can be anticipated, it is not unusual to find that offshore companies have been involved in the transactions and some of the profit
thus taken outside the UK.

The Inland Revenue is well aware of this and property transactions are the object of particular scrutiny by the investigative
branches of the Inland Revenue concerned with offshore avoidance.
The provisions of s.776 ICTA 1988 in relation to such investigations
have been dealt with in Chapter 3 above. It is worth emphasising
that, where a UK-resident individual is about to sell property in
circumstances which would give rise to an assessable capital gain,
and then decides that the gain can be sheltered by entering into an
offshore arrangement, the result may be that the transaction
becomes liable to income tax under s.776

In addition to potential exposure to s.776, all the other provisions
in relation to family trading companies previously described can
apply.

USE OF SERVICE COMPANIES/NON-OPERATION OF PAYE

In a number of circumstances, UK individuals set up non-resident
companies to supply their services in the UK. This is on the premise
that the UK user of the services will pay the non-resident company
without the operation of PAYE. The non-resident company will
then accumulate the funds in a low-tax jurisdiction. Any part of
these funds paid back to UK employees or directors is also dealt with
without the operation of PAYE. The Inland Revenue has a number
of options which it can use to challenge this arrangement. The attack
is usually on two fronts. The first is to instruct the UK user of the operations to operate PAYE. The second is then to tax the 'profit' from
the arrangement under s.739. A recent tax case (*Brackett v. Chater*
[1986] STC 521) has given strength to the Inland Revenue's argu-
ments along these lines.

In other instances, non-resident companies have been set up to
supply the services of large numbers of individuals either inside or
outside the UK. The main attraction of this has been the

non-operation of PAYE, and national insurance savings. Where such services are supplied to users in the UK, the arrangement will generally not work. The Inland Revenue usually contends that the agency legislation contained in s.134 ICTA 1988 applies, or once again will go to the underlying UK user to ask for deduction under PAYE.

SALE OF BUSINESS

There are ways in which the sale by a UK-resident individual of his business or company can be arranged to mitigate the capital gains tax arising. Unfortunately, a large part of planning in this area takes place at the last minute and under the time pressures involved in the sale of the enterprise. One way of trying to avoid a chargeable capital gain will be not to sell the assets until such time as the individual has left the country.

Such last-minute planning is unlikely to work, particularly where the individual leaves part way through a tax-year. In the recent case of *R v.CIR ex parte Fulford-Dobson* [1987] STC 344, the Inland Revenue was successful in contending that emigration from the UK to avoid capital gains tax liability constituted avoidance. This means that an individual in such a situation will be regarded as resident in the UK throughout the whole of the tax-year – contrary to the extra-statutory concession that allows taxpayers to split any year of departure and regard any period after departure as one of non-residence for capital gains tax purposes. Where, however, it can be arranged that one spouse is not resident in the UK for the whole of the tax-year in which the disposal takes place, workable planning opportunities can arise.

Another way to avoid a capital gain would be to enter into a conditional contract and ensure that the condition is not satisfied until the individual has left the UK. The date of disposal for capital gains tax purposes is the date on which the condition is satisfied.

Where an apparently conditional contract is entered into, the Inland Revenue, usually through Special Office if the sums are large, will review all the circumstances surrounding the sale. If any oral or written agreements have been entered into, it may seek to overturn the conditional contract and demonstrate that the date of disposal is earlier than the date on which the condition is satisfied and that this occurred when the vendor was resident. Alternatively, the Inland Revenue may contend that the individual is ordinarily resident at the date on which the condition is satisfied, and thus still liable to UK capital gains tax.

INDIVIDUAL'S INCOME

There are a number of instances where either self-employed individuals or individuals in employment can use non-residence or long periods spent outside the UK to extinguish completely the liability on income relating to those periods. Once again, when the sums involved are substantial, the Inland Revenue is likely to review the situation in considerable detail. In numerous cases, it finds that in practice the taxpayer has not in fact carried out the necessary steps to ensure that the income is non-taxable. The advisor may not be aware of his client's movements, e.g. when the client re-enters the UK without letting him know. The Inland Revenue's scrutiny of bank accounts, credit card statements or passports can lead to these flaws in the arrangements being highlighted.

6. REVENUE'S RESPONSE TO OFFSHORE ARRANGEMENTS

GENERAL ATTITUDE

As mentioned at the start of this book, one of the reasons for its publication is an awareness that the Inland Revenue is now taking an increasingly firm line in tackling what it perceives as abuse of offshore tax havens. Ten or fifteen years ago the Inland Revenue would not usually seek to question the legal form of arrangements, but accept these at face value. Today, particularly where offshore transactions are concerned, the Inland Revenue's general approach is one of sceptical exploration of the substance of the arrangements under review, in an attempt to demonstrate that the arrangements are not as effective as thought. Very often the Inland Revenue is proved to be right, frequently because the way in which the operations were set up, effective in theory, has not been carried through in practice. This may be because the commercial realities of the situation would never have allowed the arrangements to work, or because the taxpayer has not understood how important it is to stick to the closely defined procedures by which the aims could have been achieved.

The Inland Revenue has received additional support through the decisions of *Furniss v. Dawson* [1984] STC 153, and *Ramsay v. CIR* (1981) 54 TC 101, in that the Courts will now look at the overall picture in determining whether the substance of the arrangements is commercially valid. So the Inland Revenue may feel justified in reviewing exhaustively details of such arrangements. As its experience in the field develops, so too the Inland Revenue will have a greater pool of expertise from which to draw in tackling offshore arrangements.

Over the same period too, there has been a tendency within the Inland Revenue to concentrate its resources in specialist investigation sections, and it is worth mentioning a few in particular.

● *Special Office*

Special Offices were set up in 1976 to investigate areas where the Inland Revenue felt large amounts of tax were at risk, and where the investigation was not appropriate to other parts of the Inland Revenue. It developed particular interest in offshore arrangements, and, indeed, it has now taken on as a specific responsibility those cases where the Inland Revenue believes that

38

s.739 may be at issue. Districts are encouraged to send cases to Special Office where it appears that offshore avoidance is relevant. Other Head Office sections of the Inland Revenue will also forward cases to Special Office where its review of a specific technical point indicates that investigation may be the most appropriate way of tackling the matter. As has already been mentioned, Special Office controls the flow of information to and from foreign revenue authorities. As a consequence it has developed close links with certain of the offshore tax haven authorities.

- *Enquiry Branch*

The role of Enquiry Branch is to investigate suspected serious tax evasion, and criminal prosecution may be a possibility where this office is involved. It too has now become increasingly well informed as to the use of offshore tax haven planning, and where the arrangements are more than a case of planning having gone awry, and contain elements of tax evasion, it may well seek to take on the investigation themselves from tax districts, or, indeed, from Special Offices. Increasingly, Enquiry Branch is picking up such cases from its investigation into the role of professional advisors. It is Enquiry Branch that is responsible for the s.20C search and seize operations, of which more will be mentioned later in this chapter.

In a large number of cases, such operations involve an investigation into the role of chartered accountants, and the aim is to review working papers to make clear the reality behind uncommercial offshore invoicing arrangements, etc.

- *Special Investigation Section*

This is another Head Office unit whose role is to counter large-scale, and often off-the-shelf, tax avoidance schemes, such as those marketed by Rossminster in the mid-1970s. It also works on large projects, where the degree of research and knowledge required is such that it is not felt to be appropriate to the more direct approach of Special Offices and Enquiry Branch. To the extent that off-the-shelf avoidance schemes are now much rarer than they were a few years ago, Special Investigation Section have largely been responsible for their demise through challenges in the Courts on the substance of these arrangements.

● *Other agencies*

There are other Head Office units which are also involved in policing offshore avoidance arrangements, and of particular note is the s.770 division, part of the Inland Revenue's International Section, of which mention has been made earlier. As the name suggests it specifically reviews transfer-pricing arrangements. The International Section of the Inland Revenue is also involved in investigating international tax avoidance.

If any of the above agencies are involved in an investigation into a taxpayer's affairs, it is essential that he seek specialist advice at the earliest possible stage. Very many cases, however, start off in conventional tax districts, and inspectors around the UK are asked to be on their guard to identify use of offshore tax planning at an early stage. General guidance notes are issued to all inspectors to update them on matters of current interest, which would include developments in offshore planning. Sometimes districts may work with the specialist Inland Revenue agencies, in order to carry out fact-finding exercises without the taxpayer and his advisors being aware of the interest being taken at a higher level. All Inland Revenue enquiries on the topics considered here must therefore be taken seriously.

INLAND REVENUE METHODS

Here, primarily, the methods used by the specialist agencies are discussed, with particular reference to Special Office and Enquiry Branch, who deal more with the 'one-off' arrangements that may be of interest to the readers of this book. As indicated earlier, fact-finding is the hallmark of such Inland Revenue operations, and it is fair to say that it is increasingly difficult to satisfy the specialist agencies with an opaque reply that answers only in general terms the specific points being raised.

Considering Enquiry Branch first, it will almost invariably open its investigations by interviewing the taxpayer under what is known as the 'Hansard' extract. For these purposes, it is sufficient to say that 'Hansard' represents an inducement to disclose irregularities and cooperate with to the Inland Revenue. The 'Hansard' extract and typical formal questions initially raised are set out in Appendix 7 at the end of this book. A denial that there have been irregarities is a serious matter, because in the event that clear cut irregularities are subsequently discovered, the Inland Revenue may seek to prosecute the offender. In the event that irregularities are disclosed, the taxpayer will be asked to put flesh upon the bones of his initial disclosures by authorising the production of a report detailing the full facts about the matters of concern. Authorities from the taxpayer to approach his banks and other third parties are almost invariably sought at the opening meeting with Enquiry Branch, so that the Inland Revenue can check, without recourse to their formal information powers discussed earlier, whether the disclosure made is complete. The interview will also explore at great length the business and personal taxation history of the taxpayer, so that the Inland Revenue has a proper understanding of the background in which planning arrangements, etc., have been developed.

In the event that the taxpayer is less than forthcoming at such a meeting, and/or refuses access to business and private financial records, the Inland Revenue will see this as a failure to cooperate, and will seek to use the formal powers, described in Chapter 4 above, to obtain the information which it may seek to use to establish a prosecution position. Similarly if the completed report, following an initial disclosure, omits material matters, then the Inland Revenue may again seek to mount a criminal prosecution.

In contrast, Special Office adopts a more informal approach and often conducts the majority of its fact-finding and investigative work before confronting the taxpayer. If we consider, for example, a typical situation, where an offshore company has been inserted in a property transaction, the Special Office's approach will be to interview any and every third party from whom it can obtain information relevant to the transaction. The individuals who would be potentially likely to be approached would be vendors, purchasers, property agents, architects, planners, bankers and so on. Once again, consideration would be given to the use of the formal information powers previously described, should any resistance be met in cooperating in the supply of information, documentation, etc. At the same time, intelligence would be assembled by the use of the double taxation agreement information exchange system. In relation to a property transaction, it is worth noting, for example, that some tax-haven countries will supply details of charges registered to a particular offshore company, which can be a valuable source of information to the Inland Revenue. The result of the exhaustive investigation work carried out will normally be a detailed interview with the taxpayer whom the Inland Revenue believes to be behind the offshore arrangement, and a continuing investigation with the object of realising a settlement, which may well include tax, interest and penalties.

A similar situation would apply if the Inland Revenue was looking at an individual's own residence position, i.e. an individual who claimed that he was not resident in the UK at a particular date. Special Office would approach anybody who might have evidence to contradict this statement. For example, they would examine credit card and bank statements. They would visit clubs used by the individual, talk to neighbours and indeed even discuss the position with porters in buildings, milkmen, etc., who might have some knowledge about the comings and goings of that particular individual. Again, as mentioned above, they would be liaising with foreign revenue authorities. This could mean that, even if the UK could not tax any income or gains arising, the foreign revenue authority might have sufficient information to ensure that the individual was taxed in that country. The information obtained by the Inland Revenue in such discussions with third parties can also be of particular benefit in considering *Mareva* injunctions discussed below.

The fact-finding and research process alone can take Special Offices and Enquiry Branch many months to complete. Even after the formal opening of the case with the taxpayer and his advisors, investigations can take years, although commonly they are concluded within eighteen months to two years of their opening where effective professional advice is being used. One of the costs of investigations of this nature, which can never be quantified, is the stress that is placed on the taxpayer, particularly where his business reputation or liquidity may be put at risk by the Inland Revenue's enquiries.

ENFORCEABILITY

One of the Inland Revenue's most important powers is, of course, the ability to raise assessments where it feels that there is additional tax to be collected. The taxpayer is placed in a difficult position when assessments are raised, because the burden of proof in displacing that assessment, in other words proving that it is not valid, rests with him and not with the Inland Revenue. This is not so where assessments are raised for out-of-date years (i.e. those relevant to years more than six years before the year in which the assessment is raised). Then the Inland Revenue must be able to show that at least there has been neglect by the taxpayer. This may be an important factor in cases where interpretation of the anti-avoidance provisions alone is at issue.

The raising of the assessment, and even its determination by the appellate Commissioners (the independent arbiters on tax matters) does not, of course, mean that the Inland Revenue can necessarily enforce the consequent tax demands. This is of particular importance where offshore arrangements are being reviewed, because the Inland Revenue cannot presently enforce an assessment to tax in a foreign jurisdiction, including the Channel Islands and the Isle of Man.

Consequently, for this very practical reason, when reviewing the alternatives in relation to the typical 'one-off' avoidance scheme, the Inland Revenue's favoured options seem to be as follows:

- an assessment on a UK company in relation to the offshore profits, where the arrangements can be shown to be a complete sham;

- an assessment under s.739 on a UK individual who can be demonstrated to have been 'behind' the offshore arrangement; or

- an assessment under the agency legislation of the Taxes Acts on a UK agent. This legislation is discussed below.

ENFORCEABILITY THROUGH AN AGENT

There are machinery sections in the Taxes Management Act 1970 (e.g. ss.78, 79 and 83) which make an agent liable to tax in circumstances where a non-resident is liable through the main charging provisions of the Taxes Acts. Chief amongst these charging provisions is s.11 ICTA 1988, which relates specifically to companies, and provides that a non-resident company is to be within the charge to corporation tax if it carries on a trade through a branch or agency in the UK. In such circumstances, the agent will be liable in respect of:

- trading income of the branch;

- income from property or rights held by the branch; and

- gains arising from the disposal of assets within the UK in circumstances in which an otherwise non-resident individual would be liable to capital gains tax.

The machinery provisions could also be used to collect tax on rents derived from a UK property. This liability applies to both companies and individuals who derive UK rental income. The tax can either be collected from a UK agent, if one is used, under the machinery provisions or by deduction from the rents themselves, under s.43 ICTA 1988, if they are remitted directly abroad.

The machinery sections may also be at point where a non-resident individual or company is trading in the UK, and where no branch or agency need be involved. The charge here will be to income tax.

It should also be noted that there are provisions whereby the agent is answerable for all matters that are required to be done under the Taxes Acts. This means that, for example, the agent may become liable for interest and penalties in addition to the tax, if the circumstances warrant.

MAREVA INJUNCTIONS

One of the greatest difficulties that the UK Inland Revenue has is in collecting tax where assets have been removed from the UK jurisdiction before an assessment can be confirmed and settlement finally achieved. The Inland Revenue has therefore made occasional but increasing use of what is known as a *Mareva* injunction.

Basically, this is an injunction issued by a High Court Judge, usually in Chambers. The injunction is normally applied for by an inspector of taxes who has to show:

- the existence of an enforceable tax debt, i.e. a confirmed assessment or tax that has not been postponed; and

- an expectation that the UK Inland Revenue's position will be threatened by the removal of assets from this country.

Provided that the Court can be satisfied on both issues, an injunction will be granted, freezing the transfer of all UK assets, e.g. bank accounts, land, shares.

Because of the difficulties and time involved in such an action, the Inland Revenue is unlikely to take this course where the tax involved is less than £100,000. Where, however, such an injunction is granted, it forms a powerful inducement for the taxpayer to settle with the Inland Revenue, because he is unable to use his UK assets in any way whatsoever whilst the injunction is in existence. The immediate difficulty that the Inland Revenue has is in establishing a collectable debt quickly where it believes that assets are shortly to be removed from the country.

SEARCH AND SEIZE OPERATIONS (SECTION 20C TMA 1970)

In exceptional circumstances, where the Inland Revenue believes that major tax fraud is involved, it might proceed by its search and seize powers. While these are only used in perhaps a dozen cases a year, recent events suggest that these largely involve the use of offshore arrangements, particularly where the integrity of a professional advisor is called into question. The powers of the Inland Revenue where a warrant is granted (a Circuit Court Judge must approve the application) are enormous. The Inland Revenue can search and seize premises specified in the warrant and remove from those premises anything whatsoever, save only items for which a claim for professional privilege could be maintained and which are in the power or possession of a solicitor, barrister or advocate. Where such a warrant has been obtained and exercised, it will be the Inland Revenue's approach, if at all possible, to mount a criminal prosecution, and failing this, significant amounts of tax, interest and penalties will be sought.

There are also provisions in s.20(2) TMA 1970, which are used only rarely, and almost invariably by Special Office or Enquiry Branch. Increasingly these provisions are being invoked as quasi-s.20C powers. While they are similar to the standard information notices to the taxpayer himself under s.20(1) (and cannot be addressed to third parties), they do not require the authorisation of a Commissioner, nor do they require an informal request for the information to be provided to the taxpayer first. In other words, the Inland Revenue can, without warning, present the taxpayer with such an order with a requirement that documents be made available immediately. Failure to comply will lead to the penalty provisions of s.98 being triggered (see Chapter 4 above).

6 REVENUE AND OFFSHORE ARRANGEMENTS

THE PROFESSIONAL ADVISOR

As may have been gathered from comments made earlier in this chapter, professional advisors can be at risk where Special Office or Enquiry Branch are involved, and offshore tax-planning arrangements are the subject of its interest. In the past, particularly, it was sometimes part and parcel of the implementation of the offshore arrangements that the Inland Revenue should not become aware of the underlying facts relating to those arrangements. In other words, it was understood that if the full facts came to light, the scheme might not work, and that therefore those facts should not be made known to the Inland Revenue. If the arrangements cannot stand up under Inland Revenue scrutiny of all the relevant documents, etc., it is unsafe to advise their implementation. Moreover, if in these circumstances those documents do fall into the Inland Revenue's possession, the professional advisor himself may be at considerable risk, because he may be seen as being a party to arrangements made to defraud the Inland Revenue. In such circumstances the Inland Revenue may seek to prosecute the professional advisor, in which case all tax and working papers relating to his other clients may be obtained. Section 99 TMA 1970 should not be overlooked in this context, because, while this provides a nominal penalty of £500 maximum for knowingly inducing or assisting the making of an incorrect return or set of accounts, it too can lead to all the papers of the advisor being formally obtained.

There is an additional risk to the professional advisor, in relation to s.765 ICTA 1988, which was discussed in Chapter 3. Section 766 ICTA 1988 states that if any person is a party to an act or part of a series of acts which are unlawful under s.765, he is deemed to be guilty of an offence, and as such liable on conviction to imprisonment for not more than two years or to a fine, or to both. The Finance Act 1988 provisions regarding s.765 will, however, reduce the number of circumstances in which s.765 will apply.

7. THE CONSEQUENCES OF FAILED OFFSHORE PLANNING

The Inland Revenue's initial attack in any case that it takes up for investigation, whether or not offshore aspects are involved, is to try to ascertain whether profits, or additional profits should be assessed.

Its next step will be to ascertain whether an offence has been committed that could give rise to interest and penalties or even require criminal prosecution.

INTEREST

Interest is sought in virtually every case where there have been *omissions* or *understatements* in tax returns or accounts.

The interest provisions are at s.88 TMA 1970 and require an assessment to be made to recover tax lost through *fraud, wilful default or neglect*. It is not within the scope of this book to consider these definitions in detail. 'Neglect', the least serious of the categories, and the only one to be defined in the Taxes Management Act, is described in s.118(1) of that Act as:

> negligence or a failure to give any notice, make any return or to produce or furnish any document or other information required by or under the Taxes Acts.

So far as 'negligence' goes, it will be safe to assume that this covers any inaccuracies save those made through 'innocent error'. Where consideration of the anti-avoidance provisions discussed in this book is all that is at issue, it may be possible to show that no offence involving negligence (or fraud or wilful default) is involved.

However, as shown above, s.118(1) extends the definition of neglect beyond negligence, to include, for example, failure to give notification of liability to tax, or late submission of returns issued by the Inland Revenue, and these are often at issue in the offshore avoidance investigation. In the event that neglect (or fraud or wilful default) is proved, interest runs from the date when the tax should have been paid, had returns/accounts been correct and submitted at the proper time, until the date when the tax is actually paid.

As the interest percentage has altered over the years, a table in Appendix 8 shows the impact of interest on tax owing at any particular time.

As can be seen this can have a material effect if substantial tax is charged for earlier years.

The question of whether interest arises can be contested before the Commissioners (s.70(3)TMA 1970). However, only the Board of Inland Revenue has the power to mitigate interest charges (s.88(4)TMA 1970) and it is unusual for it to exercise that power.

PENALTIES

In investigation cases involving offshore arrangements, the penalty provisions most commonly met are those covering the submission of incorrect accounts or returns, and of failure to notify the Inland Revenue of chargeability to tax.

Where incorrect accounts or returns have been submitted, the penalties, where *neglect* is involved, are set at a maximum level of £50 per annum, plus 100% of the tax actually deemed lost.

Where *fraud* (as distinct from neglect) is involved, the maximum is £50 plus twice the amount of the tax. As mentioned earlier in relation to interest, it may be possible to show that fraud or neglect are not involved where the specific anti-avoidance provisions are all that are at issue.

Also of note and with particular relevance to offshore company arrangements, there are provisions for failing to notify the Inland Revenue of chargeability to tax within a year after the end of the year of assessment when chargeability arose. For example, the central control and management of an offshore company could be accepted after review as resting within the UK, in which case the Inland Revenue would claim penalties because the company had not notified such chargeability.

For years up to 1987/1988, penalties were set at a maximum of £100 per annum. So while the interest arising in such circumstances might be substantial, depending on the number of years involved, the penalty costs might not be large. However, the Finance Act 1988 has proposed significant changes for failure to notify chargeability and these will be relevant to the years 1988/89 onwards. Penalties in such circumstances will be set at a maximum of 100% of the tax involved in the failure. The effects of this change may be significant where, for example, a tax haven company, in truth managed and controlled from the UK, has failed to inform the Inland Revenue of its existence and chargeability to tax.

Where returns (supported by accounts) are correct but are submitted more than one year after the end of the year of assessment in which they are issued, penalties are set at a maximum of £50 per annum plus 100% of the tax involved. It is immaterial whether there has been fraud or neglect involved in the delay.

As with interest, penalties can be mitigated by the Board of Inland Revenue. While it is very unusual to achieve mitigation of interest, abatement of penalties is usually a very important feature of most investigations in negotiations with the Inland Revenue. The Inland Revenue has issued a guidance leaflet (IR 73) and the relevant part in relation to penalty abatements is set out in Appendix 9.

When abated penalties cannot be agreed, the Board of Inland Revenue can instigate formal proceedings, which it can take before the Commissioners or the High Court, where the Inland Revenue must prove the offence of fraud or neglect. If it succeeds, the decision on the amount of the penalty lies with the Commissioners or the Court (although the Board can still mitigate the amount adjudicated).

CRIMINAL PROSECUTION

Criminal prosecution for taxation fraud is rare and will usually involve cases of false accounting or returns handled by the Enquiry Branch. Even at Enquiry Branch the vast majority of cases do not result in a prosecution.

However, Enquiry Branch would generally seek to prosecute in the most serious cases, usually:

- Where a professional advisor is a party to any taxation fraud.

- Where two or more people have conspired together to defraud the Inland Revenue.

- Where false documents have been prepared to support an entry in accounts or returns.

- Where false statements, such as statements of assets or certificates of disclosure have been made, or where there has been a second serious tax offence.

- Where the taxpayer has a special status in relation to the administration of justice or of tax, e.g. a Tax Commissioner or JP.

In these cases, once the material facts have been established, the

Inland Revenue will request an interview, where questions will be put with a formal caution under the Police and Criminal Evidence Act 1984.

It is essential that legal and specialist taxation advice be sought before any such formal meeting is attended or questions answered. The Enquiry Branch's fact-finding investigation for evidence to support a prosecution may include an informal meeting where the Hansard extract is not referred to. Any such meeting needs very sensitive handling.

Finally, as mentioned earlier, where the Board's policy in regard to prosecution (the 'Hansard Extract') has been read, and no full disclosure of irregularities is made, then the Inland Revenue normally seeks a prosecution. Again, once the facts have been established, an interview under caution is usually requested.

8. DISTINGUISHING LEGAL AVOIDANCE AND EVASION – SOME ACID TESTS

The aim and thrust of this book has been to try and make those who are contemplating offshore planning more aware of the Inland Revenue's approach to such arrangements. The dividing line between legal avoidance and tax evasion is difficult to establish. The Inland Revenue is continually striving to redefine as evasion what may be seen by a taxpayer as legitimate tax planning. Without an understanding of the distinction, and what is acceptable and what is not, the taxpayer and his professional advisor are increasingly at risk.

The underlying questions that the parties to the planning must ask themselves are: 'If the Inland Revenue are given full access to all the relevant facts, does the planning have a legitimate chance of success?' Such a question should be contrasted with the question, 'Will the planning only succeed if the Inland Revenue are not given the full facts or only selected parts of the story are made available?'

The object of this book is not to close the door to offshore planning, which can and indeed will work in a large number of instances. However, in many cases, there will be a basic dilemma between the commercial reality of what actually takes place and the desire to mitigate tax under arrangements that might seem to work theoretically. It is this basic dichotomy that causes problems in offshore planning.

The taxpayer and his professional advisor must face this theoretical versus practical contradiction. Where there is no such contradiction, and planning is undertaken early, then such planning should succeed. Where, however, there is a contradiction, and planning is being undertaken at the last minute, then attempting to use a cloak of anonymity to mask or shelter the true nature of the arrangements entered into will exacerbate the risks and put the whole nature of the scheme into doubt.

The key, as in all planning, but particularly in respect of offshore planning, is to take action early and to take a realistic view of what can be achieved on a practical level. The days are long gone when the mere use of offshore arrangements or an offshore company could be thought to be sufficient to escape a UK tax liability. In such situations, the more likely outcome nowadays is a wide-ranging and successful Inland Revenue investigation. If arrangements which would now be unlikely to succeed are still in existence, then this may be the time to reappraise them to see:

- whether they are still effective; and
- if not, how they could be unwound with the minimum taxation effects.

Experience indicates that the most effective way to counter Inland Revenue interest in offshore arrangements is to seek advice from professionals who have personal experience of Inland Revenue practice and of current tax planning strategy. The Deloitte Tax Investigations Team has assembled a national group of tax investigation partners with a unique range of experience in the area of Inland Revenue investigations.

Offshore tax planning can be legitimate and tax-effective. Our tax personnel have been assembled to provide assistance to individuals or corporations who consider that their needs could legitimately benefit from the effective use of the existing taxation legislation, and they are available to consider such matters.

APPENDICES

Residence and Ordinary Residence for United Kingdom Tax Puposes

General

6   The terms "resident" and "ordinarily resident" are not defined in the United Kingdom Income Tax Acts, but guidance as to the meaning of these words has been given in decisions by the Court. These show that both expressions are used in their everyday sense and do not have any special or technical meaning. The term "domicile", on the other hand, is always used in its strictly legal sense. (See paras. 31-35 *[not reproduced]*.)

7   In the Income Tax Acts, "resident" and "ordinarily resident" are always used to describe a situation arising in a tax year, and not in relation to some longer or shorter period. The question that generally has to be decided is whether or not a person is resident (or ordinarily resident) in the United Kingdom in a particular tax year. It is not practicable to do more in this booklet than set out the main principles which are followed in answering this question because each case depends on its particular facts.

8   If a person is to be regarded as resident in the United Kingdom for a given tax year he must normally be physically present in the country for at least part of that year. He will always be resident if he is here for six months or more in the year. **There are no exceptions to this rule.** Six months is regarded as equivalent to 183 days, whether or not the year is a leap year. For this purpose a count is made of the total number of days spent in the United Kingdom during the year whether the stay is out of one period only or a succession of visits. Under present practice days of arrival and days of departure are normally ignored. If the person is here for less than six months, the decision whether or not he is resident depends on other circumstances (see paragraphs 13-30).

9   "Ordinarily resident" is broadly equivalent to habitually resident; if a person is resident in the United Kingdom year after year, he is ordinarily resident here. It follows that a person may be resident but not ordinarily resident in the United Kingdom for a given tax year—if, for instance, he normally lives outside the United Kingdom but visits here in that year for six months or more. Or he may be ordinarily resident but not resident for a given tax year—if, for instance, he usually lives in the United Kingdom but has gone abroad for a long holiday and does not set foot in the United Kingdom during that year.

10 A person may be resident (or ordinarily resident) in two or more countries at the same time. He cannot claim to be not resident (or not ordinarily resident) in the United Kingdom merely because in that tax year he is resident (or ordinarily resident) in another country. Where, however, a person is regarded as resident both in the United Kingdom and in a country with which the United Kingdom has a double taxation agreement there may be special provisions in the agreement for treating the person as a resident of only one of the countries for purposes of the agreement.

11 Strictly speaking, each tax year must be looked at as a whole, and a person is to be treated as either resident or not resident for the whole year: he cannot be regarded as resident for part of the year and not resident for the remainder. Thus a person who is ordinarily resident in the United Kingdom and who goes abroad for a period which does not include a *complete* tax year (e.g. if he was abroad for the period from July 1981 to March 1983) is regarded as remaining resident and ordinarily resident throughout. But it is the practice, by concession, to split the year if the person:—

(a) is a new permanent resident, provided that he has been not ordinarily resident in the United Kingdom; or

(b) has left the United Kingdom for permanent residence abroad, provided that he becomes not ordinarily resident in the United Kingdom; or

(c) subject to certain condtions (see paragraph 18) is taking full-time employment abroad.

Where the tax year is split in this way, the day of departure from, or arrival in, the United Kingdom falls into the period of residence and ordinary residence here.

Husband and Wife

12 A wife's residence and ordinary residence status is not governed by her husband's status but is determined by her own circumstances. If, for example, a husband is employed abroad full-time and his wife goes out to join him, but later returns to the United Kingdom without having been away for a complete tax year, she is regarded as remaining resident and ordinarily resident here although he may be not resident and not ordinarily resident. If the residence status of husband and wife differ they may be treated as separate persons for tax purposes if it is to their advantage. (See para. 83 [*not reproduced*].)

Leaving the United Kingdom

13 A person who has been ordinarily resident here is treated as remaining resident and ordinarily resident if he goes abroad for short periods only.

14 If a person goes abroad permanently but has accommodation (e.g. a house or apartment) available for his use in the United Kingdom, he is regarded as resident here for any tax year in which he visits the United Kingdom, however short the visit may be: and he is regarded as remaining ordinarily resident if he comes here in most years. The circumstances in which accommodation is regarded as available are set out in paragraphs 28 to 30.

15 Even if a person who has taken up permanent residence abroad has no accommodation available in the United Kingdom he is regarded as continuing to be resident and ordinarily resident here if he returns here for periods which amount to an *average* of three months or more per tax year.

16 If a person claims that he has ceased to be resident and ordinarily resident in the United Kingdom, and can produce some evidence for this (for example that he has sold his house here and set up a permanent home abroad), his claim may be admitted provisionally with effect from the day following his departure. Normally this provisional ruling is confirmed after he has remained abroad for a period which includes a complete tax year and during which any visits to this country have not amounted to an annual average of three months or more a year.

17 If, however, he cannot produce sufficient evidence, a decision on his claim will be postponed for three years and will then be made by reference to what actually happened in that period. During the intervening tax years, his tax liability is computed provisionally on the basis that he remains resident in the United Kingdom. He therefore continues to receive the various income tax reliefs due to the resident of the United Kingdom (see paragraph 59 [*not reproduced*]) except for any tax year in which he does not set foot in the United Kingdom. His liability is adjusted, if necessary, when the final decision is made at the end of three years.

18 If a person goes abroad for full-time service under a contract of employment and;—

(*a*) all the duties of his employment are performed abroad or any duties he performs here are incidental to his duties abroad (see paragraphs 37-39); and

(*b*) his absence from the United Kingdom and the employment itself is for a period which includes a complete tax year; and

(*c*) interim visits to the United Kingdom during the period do not amount to (i) six months or more in any one tax year or (ii) an average of three months or more per tax year,

he is normally regarded as not resident and not ordinarily resident in the United Kingdom from the day following the date of his departure until the day preceding the date of his return. On his return he is regarded as a new permanent resident.

Coming to the United Kingdom
New permanent residents

19 A person whose home has previously been abroad and who comes to the United Kingdom to take up permanent residence here is regarded as resident and ordinarily resident from the date of his arrival.

Visitors—General

20 A person whose home is abroad and who comes to the United Kingdom only as a visitor will not be treated as resident or ordinarily resident here except in the circumstances described in the following paragraphs.

21 As mentioned in paragraph 8, a visitor who stays for six months in a tax year will always be regarded as resident here. A visitor who has accommodation available here will be regarded as resident for any year in which he comes to the United Kingdom, however short his visit may be (but see paragraphs 29 and 30 below): if he visits in four or more consecutive tax years, or intends to do so, he will be treated as ordinarily resident also. A visitor who has no accommodation available will be regarded as becoming resident and ordinarily resident after his visits for four consecutive tax years have averaged three months or more per tax year. If it is clear when he first comes that he proposes to make such visits, he may be treated as resident and ordinarily resident in the United Kingdom from the start. A person who only visits the United Kingdom occasionally will not become ordinarily resident, but he will be resident for any tax year in which his visits amount to six months or more in aggregate.

22 The general principles described above are applied in the case of *all* visitors to the United Kingdom. There are additional principles applicable to certain special categories, and these are set out in the following paragaphs.

Visits for education

23 A person who comes to the United Kingdom for a period of study or education which is expected to last for more than four years will be regarded as resident and ordinarily resident from the date of his arrival. If the period is not expected to exceed four years, he may be treated as not ordinarily resident, but this will depend on whether

(a) he has accommodation available here (see paragraph 28); or

(b) he intends to remain here at the end of his period of education; or

(c) he proposes to visit the United Kingdom in future years for average annual periods of three months or more per tax year.

If, despite the original expectation, he remains in the United Kingdom for more than four years, he will be treated in any event as ordinarily resident as from the beginning of the fifth tax year of his stay. His residence position will in any case be decided on the lines set out in paragraph 21.

24 If a parent or guardian of a child comes to the United Kingdom in connection with the child's education, the practice described in paragraph 23 is also applied to him.

Visits for temporary employment

25 A person who comes to the United Kingdom to work for a period of at least two years is treated as resident here for the whole period from the day of arrival to the day of departure. In general, any other person coming to this country for employment will not be treated as resident unless he spends six months or more here in a tax year, or unless he has accommodation available (see paragraph 28). His ordinary residence status will normally follow the rules in paragraphs 26 and 27 below.

Visits for prolonged or indefinite residence

26 A person who comes to the United Kingdom, whether to work here or not, will be ordinarily resident from the date of his arrival if it is clear that he intends to remain here for three years or more. If he has no definite intention as to the length of his stay and does not have accommodation in the United Kingdom available for his use (see paragraph 27), he may be regarded as ordinarily resident from the beginning of the tax year in which the third anniversary of his arrival falls. A person who does not decide to stay here permanently until he has been here for a little while is normally regarded as ordinarily resident from the beginning of the tax year in which he takes that decision.

27 In addition it is the general practice to regard someone who comes to the United Kingdom as ordinarily resident for tax purposes:

(a) from the date of arrival if he has or acquires during the year of arrival, accommodation for his use in the United Kingdom which he occupies on a basis that implies a stay in this country of three years or more; or

(b) from the beginning of the tax year in which such accommodation becomes available.

If a person, who has been regarded as ordinarily resident solely because he has accommodation here, disposes of the accommodation and leaves the United Kingdom within 3 years of his arrival he may be treated as not ordinarily resident for the duration of his stay if this is to his advantage.

Available accommodation

28 Where a person's residence or ordinary residence position turns on whether or not he has accommodation available for his use, the question is whether any accommodation is *in fact* available for his use. For this purpose ownership is immaterial—a person does not have to own or rent a house, apartment or other accommodation for it to be available for his use; contrariwise, a house he owns and lets out on a lease under the terms of which he has no right or permission to stay in it will be ignored. A house owned or rented by one spouse will usually be considered available for the use of the other. But any accommodation rented for use during a temporary stay here may be ignored if the period of renting is less than two years for furnished accommodation or one year for unfurnished accommodation.

29 Even if there is accommodation available for his use, it may be ignored if the person is working full-time in a business, profession or employment carried on wholly abroad. But such accommodation is *not* ignored where the person owns a business, or is a partner in a business, carried on mainly abroad but which has a branch or permanent establishment in the United Kingdom; and this is so even though he himself does not work here.

30 If a person is employed abroad and some of his duties are performed in the United Kingdom it may be possible to ignore available accommodation provided that his duties in the United Kingdom are merely incidental to his duties abroad; the circumstances in which duties are regarded as merely incidental to the main duties of the employment are outlined in paragraphs 37 to 39 [*not reproduced*].

APPENDIX 2. COMPANY RESIDENCE

INLAND REVENUE STATEMENT OF PRACTICE SP6/83, 27 JULY 1983

1 Residence has always been a material factor, for companies as well as individuals, in determining tax liability. But statute law has never laid down any general rules for determining where a company is resident. The question has thus been left to the Courts to decide.

The case law test

2 The test of company residence is that enunciated by Lord Loreburn in *De Beers Consolidated Mines v Howe* 5 TC 198 at the beginning of this century—

> "A company resides, for the purposes of Income Tax, where its real business is carried on . . . I regard that as the true rule; and the real business is carried on where the central management and control actually abides."

3 The "central management and control" test, as set out in *De Beers*, has been endorsed by a series of subsequent decisions. In particular, it was described by Lord Radcliffe in the 1959 case of *Bullock v Unit Construction Company* 38 RC 712 at page 738 as being—

> "as precise and unequivocal as a positive statutory injunction . . . I do not know of any other test which has either been substituted for that of central management and control, or has been defined with sufficient precision to be regarded as an acceptable alternative to it. To me . . . it seems impossible to read Lord Loreburn's words without seeing that he regarded the formula he was propounding as constituting *the* test of residence".

Nothing which has happened since has in any way altered this basic principle: under current UK case law a company is regarded as resident for tax purposes where central management and control is to be found.

Place of "central management and control"

4 In determining whether or not an individual company is resident in the UK, it thus becomes necessary to locate its place of "central management and control". The case law concept of central management and control is, in broad terms, directed at the highest level of control of the business of a company. It is to be distinguished from the place where the main operations of a business are to be found, though those two places may often coincide. Moreover, the exercise of control does not necessarily demand any minimum standard of active involvement: it may, in appropriate circumstances, be exercised tacitly through passive oversight.

5 Successive decided cases have emphasised that the place of central management and control is wholly a question of fact. For example, Lord Radcliffe in *Unit Construction* said that "the question where control and management abide must be treated as one of fact or 'actuality' " (p 741). It follows that factors which together are decisive in one instance may individually carry little weight in another. Nevertheless the decided cases do give some pointers. In particular a series of decisions has attached importance to the place where the company's board of directors meet. There are very many cases in which the board meets in the same country as that in which the business operations take place, and central management and control is clearly located in that one place. In other cases central management and control may be exercised by directors in one country though the actual business operations may, perhaps under the immediate management of local directors, take place elsewhere.

6 But the location of board meetings, although important in the normal case, is not necessarily conclusive. Lord Radcliffe in *Unit Construction* pointed out (p 738) that the site of the meetings of the directors' board had *not* been chosen as "*the* test" of company residence. In some cases, for example, central management and control is exercised by a single individual. This may happen when a chairman or managing director exercises powers formally conferred by the company's Articles and the other board members are little more than cyphers, or by reason of a dominant shareholding or for some other reason. In those cases the residence of the company is where the controlling individual exercises his powers.

7 In general the place of directors' meetings is significant only in so far as those meetings constitute the medium through which central management and control is exercised. If, for example, the directors of a company were engaged together actively in the UK in the complete running of a business which was wholly in the UK, the company would not be regarded as resident outside the UK merely because the directors held formal board meetings outside the UK. While it is possible to identify extreme situations in which central management and control plainly is, or is not, exercised by directors in formal meetings, the conclusion in any case is wholly one of fact depending on the relative weight to be given to various factors. Any attempt to lay down rigid guidelines would only be misleading.

8 Generally, however, where doubts arise about a particular company's residence status, the Revenue adopt the following approach—

(i) They first try to ascertain whether the directors of the company in fact exercise central management and control.

(ii) If so, they seek to determine where the directors exercise this central management and control (which is not necessarily where they meet).

(iii) In cases where the directors apparently do *not* exercise central management and control of the company, the Revenue then look to establish where and by whom it is exercised.

Parent/subsidiary relationship

9 It is particularly difficult to apply the "central management and control" test in the situation where a subsidiary company and its parent operate in different territories. In this situation, the parent will normally influence, to a greater or lesser extent, the actions of the subsidiary. Where that influence is exerted by the parent exercising the powers which a sole or majority shareholder has in general meetings of the subsidiary, for example to appoint and dismiss members of the board of the subsidiary and to initiate or approve alterations to its financial structure, the Revenue would not seek to argue that central management and control of the subsidiary is located where the parent company is resident. However, in cases where the parent usurps the functions of the board of the subsidiary (such as *Unit Construction* itself) or where that board merely rubber stamps the parent company's decisions without giving them any independent consideration of its own, the Revenue draw the conclusion that the subsidiary has the same residence for tax purposes as its parent.

10 The Revenue recognise that there may be many cases where a company is a member of a group having its ultimate holding company in another country which will not fall readily into either of the categories referred to above. In considering whether the board of such a subsidiary company exercises central management and control of the subsidiary's business they have regard to the degree of autonomy which those directors have in conducting the company's business. Matters (among others) that may be taken into account are the extent to which the directors of the subsidiary take decisions on their own authority as to investment, production, marketing and procurement without reference to the parent.

Double taxation agreements

11 In general our double taxation agreements do not affect the UK residence of a company as established for UK tax purposes. But where the partner country adopts a different definition of residence, it may happen that a UK resident company is treated, under the partner country's domestic law, as also resident there. In these cases, the agreement normally specifies what the tax consequences of this "double" residence shall be.

12 Under the double taxation agreement with the United States, for example, the UK residence of a company for UK tax purposes is unaffected. But where that company is also a US corporation, it is excluded from some of the reliefs conferred by the agreement. On the other hand, under a double taxation agreement which follows the 1977 OECD Model Taxation Convention, a company classed as resident by both the UK and the partner country is, for the purposes of the agreement, treated as resident where its "place of effective management" is situated.

13 The Commentary in paragraph 3 of Article 4 of the OECD Model records the UK view that, in agreements (such as those with some Commonwealth countries) which treat a company as resident in a state in which "its business is managed and controlled", this expression means "the effective management of the enterprise". More detailed consideration of the question in the light of the approach of Continental legal systems and of Community law to the question of company residence has led the Revenue to revise this view. It is now considered that effective management may, in some cases, be found at a place different from the place of central management and control. This could happen, for example, where a company is run by executives based abroad, but the final directing power rests with non-executive directors who meet in the UK. In such circumstances the company's place of effective management might well be abroad but, depending on the precise powers of the non-executive directors, it might be centrally managed and controlled (and therefore resident) in the UK.

Conclusion

14 In outlining factors relevant to the application of the case law test, this statement assumes that they exist for genuine commercial reasons. Where, however, as may happen, it appears that a major objective underlying the existence of certain factors is the obtaining of tax benefits from residence or non-residence, the Revenue examines the facts particularly closely in order to see whether there has been an attempt to create the appearance of central management and control in a particular place without the reality.

15 The test examined in this statement is not always easy to apply in present day circumstances. The last relevant case was decided over 20 years ago, and there have been many developments in communications since then, which in particular may enable a company to be controlled from a place far distant from where the day-to-day management is carried on. As the statement makes clear, while the general principle has been laid down by the Courts, its application must depend on the precise facts.

INLAND REVENUE GUIDANCE NOTES ON S.485 ICTA 1970
[S.770 ICTA 1988], 26 JANUARY 1981

1 *Introduction*

These notes are primarily designed for the guidance of overseas companies which have, or may be thinking of setting up, subsidiaries in the UK; but the law and practice described apply to UK resident companies generally.

2 *General—the arm's length principle*

Prices charged in transactions between connected companies in a multinational group (transfer prices) may be designed to meet the convenience of the group as a whole. They will not necessarily produce a figure of profit or loss which can be accepted for tax purposes. The UK law therefore, in common with that of many other countries, provides that these prices may be adjusted in arriving at the taxable profit or allowable loss of a UK taxpayer. The price to which they may be adjusted is the "arm's length price". This is the price which might have been expected if the parties to the transaction had been independent persons dealing at arm's length i.e. dealing with each other in a normal commercial manner unaffected by any special relationship between them.

3 *Circumstances in which adjustments may be made to transfer prices*

The relevant law is largely contained in TA 1970, S.485 *[S.770 ICTA 1988]*. This provides the Inland Revenue with power, for example, to adjust a transfer price to the arm's length price in transactions between a resident and a non-resident body of persons when one controls the other or both are under common control.

4 *Body of persons*

A "body of persons" includes a partnership as well as a company.

5 *Residence of a company*

The general rule is that a company is resident where the central control and management of its trade or business is carried on. The application of the rule is a question of fact.

6 *Control of a company*

Control of a company has to be distinguished from the control and management of its trade or business. For the purposes of S. 485 it is defined in particular to mean, as in TA 1970, S.534 *[S.840 ICTA*

1988], the power of a person to secure that the affairs of the company are conducted in accordance with his wishes, *inter alia*, by holding shares or possessing voting power in relation to that company (or any other company) or by virtue of any powers conferred by the articles of association or other document regulating that or any other company.

7 *Scope of UK transfer pricing law*

S. 485 applies to sales of goods and other property, lettings or hiring of property, grants and transfers of rights, interests and licences and the giving of business facilities of whatever kind. Loan interest, patent royalties, management fees, and payments for services are thus within its scope as well as payments for goods. Contributions by a subsidiary towards costs incurred by the parent company are similarly within its scope.

8 *Tax returns—assessment of profits—onus of proof—rights of appeal*

The UK system of taxing profits requires the taxpayer to make a return of his profits each year to the appropriate Inspector of Taxes. It is normal for his return to be accompanied by accounts and computations in some detail in order to substantiate the return. But the inspector, if no return is made or if he is dissatisfied with a return which has been made, is however empowered to assess the liability of tax on the basis of his own estimate of the profits. The taxpayer has a right of appeal to independent Commissioners (and from the Commissioners, on a point of law, to the High Court and beyond) but it is for him in the first instance to disprove the correctness of the assessment in such an appeal and not for the inspector to prove that it is correct.

9 *Adjustment by agreement*

If, however, the Inspector takes the view that it may be necessary to assess the profits on the basis of his own estimate he will normally seek, in any case where substantial amounts are at stake, to come to an agreement on the matter with the taxpayer either by correspondence or, very probably in a case where the adjustment of transfer prices is in point, by discussion round the table as well.

10 *Requests for information*

If it seems to the Inspector that it may be necessary to adjust a company's transfer prices for tax purposes he will normally, therefore, in the first place, ask the UK company for the information necessary to decide whether adjustments should be made and what sort of adjustments. There is no standard list of questions—each case will need to be looked at in the light of its own special features. But the inspector will generally be interested in such matters as who owns or controls the company, what the nature of the trade is, how any group of which the company is a member is organised, what are the functions of particular companies in the group, what the results of the UK companies have been, how far they have come up to expectations and so on. The need for answers to more detailed questions may emerge as the discussions proceed.

11 *Powers to require information*
The Inland Revenue have power in certain circumstances to require the production of information for tax purposes and, in particular under FA 1975, S. 17 *[S.772 ICTA 1988]*, they may require a company to produce information which is relevant to the adjustment of transfer prices (not necessarily its own transfer prices) under TA 1970, S. 485. Powers provided under S. 17 also include in certain circumstances the power to require the production of information (including books and accounts) from a UK resident company, which is relevant to transactions with a 51% subsidiary resident outside the UK including books and accounts of the subsidiary. This also applies where the transactions are between UK resident and non-resident companies both of which are 51% subsidiaries of the UK resident company. (The UK parent company may however appeal against the requirement to an independent body of Commissioners.) In addition, in certain circumstances the Board may require books and accounts and other documents or records which are relevant to a transfer pricing adjustment under S. 485 to be produced for examination by an Inspector of Taxes on the taxpayer's premises.

12 *Confidentiality*
Officers of the Inland Revenue are governed by very strict rules about the confidentiality of information received by them in the course of their duties. They are prohibited from disclosing such information except for tax purposes and, within that limitation, in very limited circumstances strictly defined by law.

13 *Exchange of information with other countries*
Disclosure is permitted (under strict safeguards) to other countries' tax authorities under agreements for the relief of double taxation

and under the Directive concerning mutual assistance between tax authorities of the member States of the European Communities. (The Inland Revenue may also receive information from other countries under these instruments.)

14 *Inland Revenue Organisation*
The Inland Revenue maintains a network of local tax offices spread over the whole of the UK and normally the affairs of a taxpayer will be mainly dealt with by a local Inspector of Taxes. But transfer pricing problems involving substantial amounts of money or important matters of principle may be dealt with instead by a section of the central head office in London. (The affairs of oil companies including matters of transfer pricing are dealt with by a centralised Oil Taxation Office in London.)

15 *Objectives and methods of approach in adjusting transfer prices for tax purposes*
The objective of both central and local offices are however the same. The principal objective is to ensure that the UK taxpayer is paying the proper UK tax on its profits under the law. The Inland Revenue recognise, however, that answering the many detailed questions which may be necessary for the achievement of this objective may impose an onerous burden on the senior staff of companies or their advisers and they aim to keep these questions to a minimum by concentrating on the main pricing issues involved.

16 *Methods of and considerations taken into account in arriving at arm's length prices*
In ascertaining an arm's length price the Inland Revenue will often look for evidence of prices in similar transactions between parties who are in fact operating at arm's length. They may however find it more useful in some circumstances to start with the re-sale price of the goods or services etc. and arrive at the relevant arm's length purchase price by deducting an appropriate mark up. They may find it more convenient on the other hand to start with the cost of the goods or services and arrive at the arm's length price by adding an appropriate mark up. But they will in practice use any method which seems likely to produce a satisfactory result. They will be guided in their search for an arm's length price by the considerations set out in the OECD Report on Multinationals and Transfer Pricing. (This Report examines the considerations which need to be

taken into account in arriving at arm's length prices in general and also in particular in the context of sales of goods, the provision of intra group services, the transfer of technology and rights to use trademarks within a group and the provision of intra group loans.)

17 *Settlement of problems*
The Inland Revenue recognise, as does the OECD Report, that the evidence needed to establish an arm's length price may be hard to come by and difficult to interpret and they recognise also that decisions on pricing in the arm's length situation would have had to be taken in the light of the facts which could have been known at the time when the decision was made. It is with considerations like this in mind that they are concerned to settle transfer pricing adjustments as far as possible by discussion and agreement with the companies concerned. They would hope as a result also to establish a reasonable basis of understanding with the companies for the future (possibly on the basis of a review after a number of years).

18 *Consultation with other countries*
The Inland Revenue recognise that transfer pricing adjustments may have a consequence not only for UK tax but also for foreign tax. They are able, under the terms of some seventy agreements for the relief of double taxation and the prevention of fiscal evasion, to exchange information with the tax authorities of their partner countries on transfer pricing matters among others and they often do this for the purpose of ensuring that tax is adequately charged in the UK. On the other hand, they are also able to consult and do consult with partner countries with a view to preventing unrelievable double taxation arising from (among other causes) the adjustment of transfer prices. A taxpayer who fears that unrelievable double taxation may result in his own case from some action of the tax authorities of a treaty partner may ask the UK Inland Revenue to enter into such consultations and they will do so whenever the need arises. All that such a taxpayer need do is to write a letter putting his request, and giving the relevant details, to the International Tax Policy Division of the Inland Revenue in Somerset House, London. For such consultation to be effective however it will usually be necessary for the request to be made in good time so as not to be frustrated by the expiry of legal time limits for tax adjustments either in the UK or in the other country.

19 *Time limits for claims for credit*
So far as concerns claiming relief for foreign tax against UK tax the normal rule is that a claim in respect of any income, must be made not later than six years from the end of the chargeable period for which the income is chargeable to UK tax. However where such credit has been rendered insufficient by reason of an adjustment to the other country's tax the time limit for a claim to additional credit is six years from the time when the adjustment was made—TA 1970, S. 512 [*S.806 ICTA 1988*].

20 *Status of these notes*
These notes are for guidance only. They express the Inland Revenue's view of the law but they have no legal force and they do not affect any rights of appeal on points concerning a taxpayer's liability. Similarly any description in these notes of Inland Revenue approaches to the problem of transfer pricing or practices in dealing with this problem are not to be taken as limiting the Department to such approaches or practices in any particular case.

APPENDIX 4. PUBLIC RECORD INFORMATION IN TAX HAVEN COUNTRIES

BERMUDA

	Are records public?	Location of records
Court records	Yes	Supreme Court Building
Wills	Yes	Supreme Court Building
Patents	Yes	Registrar General
Trademarks	Yes	Registrar General
Copyrights	Yes	Registrar General
Commercial register	Yes	Registrar of Cos.
Company register	Yes	Registrar of Cos.
Land transfer records	Yes	Registrar General
Birth records	Yes	Registrar General
Death records	Yes	Registrar General
Marriage records	Yes	Registrar General
Bank information	Not available	
Credit information	Yes	Bermuda Credit Association
Company records	Yes	Registrar of Cos.
Company by-laws	Not available	
Company financial statements	Not available	

CHANNEL ISLANDS – JERSEY

Court records	Yes	Judicial Greffier
Wills	Yes	Judicial Greffier
Patents	Yes	Commercial Relations Dept.
Trademarks	Yes	Commercial Relations Dept.
Copyrights	None filed in Jersey – UK registration applies	
Commercial register	Yes	Commercial Relations Dept.
Company register	Yes	Commercial Relations Dept.
Land transfer records	Yes	Judicial Greffier
Birth records	Yes	Superintendent Registrar
Death records	Yes	Superintendent Registrar
Marriage records	Yes	Superintendent Registrar
Bank information	Not available	
Credit information	Not available	
Company records	Yes	Commercial Relations Dept.
Company by-laws	Yes	Commercial Relations Dept.
Company financial statements	Not available	

CHANNEL ISLANDS – ALDERNEY	Are records public?	Location of records
Court records	Yes	Clerk of Court
Wills	Yes	Clerk of Court
Patents	None in Alderney	
Trademarks	None in Alderney	
Copyrights	None in Alderney	
Commercial register	None in Alderney	
Company register	Yes	Clerk of Court
Land transfer records	Yes	Clerk of Court
Birth records	Yes	Clerk of Court
Death records	Yes	Clerk of Court
Marriage records	Yes	Clerk of Court
Bank information	Not available	
Credit information	Not available	
Company records	Yes	Clerk of Court
Company by-laws	Yes	Clerk of Court
Company financial statements	Not available	

CHANNEL ISLANDS – GUERNSEY

Court records	Yes	Her Majesty's Greffier
Wills	Yes	Her Majesty's Greffier
Patents	None filed in Guernsey	
Trademarks	Yes	Her Majesty's Greffier
Copyrights	None filed in Guernsey	
Commercial register	Yes	Her Majesty's Greffier
Company register	Yes	Her Majesty's Greffier
Land transfer records	Yes	Her Majesty's Greffier
Birth records	Yes	Her Majesty's Greffier
Death records	Yes	Her Majesty's Greffier
Marriage records	Yes	Her Majesty's Greffier
Bank information	Not available	
Credit information	Not available	
Company records	Yes	Her Majesty's Greffier
Company by-laws	Yes	Her Majesty's Greffier
Company financial statements	Not available	

CAYMAN ISLANDS	Are records public?	Location of records
Court records	Yes	Courts Office Building
Wills	Yes	Courts Office Building
Patents	Yes	Administration Building
Trademarks	Yes	Administration Building
Copyrights	Yes	Administration Building
Commercial register	Not available	
Company register	No	Office of Registrar
Land transfer records	Yes	Land Survey Office
Birth records	Yes	Courts Office Building
Death records	Yes	Courts Office Building
Marriage records	Yes	Courts Office Building
Bank information	Not available	
Credit information	Not available	
Company records	No	Administration Building
Company by-laws	No	Administration Building
Company financial statements	Not available	

LIECHTENSTEIN		
Court records	No	Landgericht
Wills	No	Landgericht
Patents	Yes	Amt für Geistiges Eigentum
Trademarks	Yes	Amt für Volkswirtschaft
Copyrights	Yes	Amt für Geistiges Eigentum
Commercial register	Yes	Handelsregister Landgericht
Company register	No	Handelsregister Landgericht
Land transfer records	No	Grundbuchamt
Birth records	Yes	Liechtensteinisches Zivilstandsa
Death records	Yes	Zivilstandsamt
Marriage records	Yes	Zivilstandsamt
Bank information	Not available	
Credit information	No	Auskunftei Agal Aeulestr.
Company records	No	Handelsregister Landgericht
Company by-laws	Not available	
Company financial statements	No	Handelsregister Landgericht

ISLE OF MAN	Are records public?	Location of records
Court records	Yes	General Registry
Wills	Yes	General Registry
Patents	No	
Trademarks	No	
Copyrights	No	
Commercial register	Yes	General Registry
Company register	Yes	Registry of Companies
Land transfer records	Yes	General Registry
Birth records	Yes	Registrar of Births, Deaths, Marriages
Death records	Yes	
Marriage records	Yes	
Bank information	Not available	
Credit information	Not available	
Company records	Yes	Registry of Companies
Company by-laws	Yes	Registry of Companies
Company financial statements	Not available	

LUXEMBOURG		
Court records	No	Casier Judiciaire
Wills	No	Notaire for the Estate
Patents	Yes	Ministry of Economic Affairs
Trademarks	Yes	Ministry of Economic Affairs
Copyrights	Yes	Ministry of Economic Affairs
Commercial register	Yes	Registre Central des Sociétés
Company register	Yes	Registre Central des Sociétés
Land transfer records	Yes	City Hall
Birth records	Yes	City Registrar
Death records	Yes	City Registrar
Marriage records	No	City Registrar
Bank information	Not available	
Credit information	No	Banks
Company records	Yes	Service Central de Législation
Company by-laws	Yes	Registre Central des Sociétés
Company financial statements	Yes	Registre Central des Sociétés

NETHERLANDS ANTILLES	Are records public?	Location of records
Court records	Yes	Justice Department
Wills	Yes	Civil Registration Department
Patents	Yes	Trademark Bureau
Trademarks	Yes	Trademark Bureau
Copyrights	Yes	Trademark Bureau
Commercial registrar	No records	
Company register	Yes	Curaçao Chamber of Commerce
Land transfer records	Yes	Government Land Registry Offic
Birth records	Yes	Civil Registry
Death records	Yes	Civil Registry
Marriage records	Yes	Civil Registry
Bank information	Not available	
Credit information	No records	
Company records	Yes	Curaçao Chamber of Commerce
Company by-laws	Yes	Curaçao Chamber of Commerce
Company financial statetments	Not available	

SWITZERLAND

Court records	No	Central Police Office
Wills	No	Office of the Attorney or Notary
Patents	Yes	Fed. Office for Intellectual Prope
Trademarks	Yes	Fed. Office for Intellectual Prope
Copyrights	Yes	Fed. Office for Intellectual Prope
Commercial register	Yes	Office for Trade & Goods Registr
Company register	Yes	Office for Trade & Goods Registr
Land transfer records	Yes	Office of the Registrar
Birth records	Yes	Federal Office of Civil Records
Death records	Yes	Federal Office of Civil Records
Marriage records	Yes	Federal Office of Civil Records
Bank information	Not available	
Credit information	Yes	Private Credit Agencies
Company records	Not available	
Company by-laws	Not available	
Company financial statements	Yes	Commercial Register in each Car

PANAMA	Are records public?	Location of records
Court records	Yes	Judicial Dept. Registry
Wills	Yes	Judicial Dept. Registry
Patents	Yes	Judicial Dept. Registry
Trademarks	Yes	Judicial Dept. Registry
Copyrights	Yes	Judicial Dept. Registry
Commercial register	No	Judicial Dept. Registry
Company register	Yes	Registrar's Office
Land transfer records	Yes	Registrar's Office
Birth records	Yes	Registro Civil
Death records	Yes	Registro Civil
Marriage records	Not available	
Bank information	Not available	
Credit information	No	Panamanian Credit Assoc.
Company records	Not available	
Company by-laws	Yes	Registrar's Office
Company financial statements	Not available	

SARK		
Court records	No	
Wills	No	
Patents	No	
Trademarks	No	
Copyrights	No	
Commercial register	No	
Company register	No	
Land transfer records	Yes	Greffe
Birth records	Yes	Greffe
Death records	Yes	Greffe
Marriage records	Yes	Greffe
Bank information	No	
Credit information	No	
Company records	No	
Company by-laws	No	
Company financial statements	No	

INCOME TAX (INCLUDING SURTAX)

NOTICE UNDER SECTION 745(1) OF THE
INCOME AND CORPORATION TAXES ACT 1988

1. The Commissioners of Inland Revenue in exercise of their powers
    under Section 745(1) of the Income and Corporation Taxes Act
    1988 hereby require you to furnish to them on or before
    at the address given above the particulars indicated in paragraphs
    3-9 below.

Interpretation

2. For the purposes of this Notice (and of the following definitions) –

    (a) 'assets' includes property or rights of any kind (including
         rights in connection with the provision of services);

    (b) 'company' includes any body corporate and any legal
         person which is treated as a body corporate for tax purposes
         by the law of a country in which according to the law of that
         country for any purpose it is, or is deemed to be, situate or
         resident;

    (c) 'the Companies' means *A. Enterprise Ltd* and *B. Investments
         Ltd*;

    (d) 'interest' includes a future or contingent interest and an
         option to acquire an interest; and a person shall be treated as
         having an interest in a trust or settlement if that person may
         directly or indirectly receive any benefit from the exercise of
         one or more powers or discretions under such trust or
         settlement;

    (e) 'person' includes any company, partnership or firm and,
         without prejudice to the foregoing, includes any legal person
         recognised by the law of a country in which according to the
         law of that country for any purpose it is, or is deemed to be,
         situate or resident;

    (f) 'public unit trust' means a trust holding itself open for
         investment by the general public;

    (g) 'quoted company' means a company whose shares are
         quoted on a recognised stock exchange;

    (h) 'trust' includes any family foundation or other institution
         the regulating provisions of which provide for assets or

income to be held or applied wholly or in part of the benefit of individuals or for other family or private purposes; but does not (except where the term is used) include a public unit trust; and

references to the transfer of assets include transfers by way of sale, gift, loan, purchase consideration, subscription for shares, or otherwise.

Information required

3. (a) Particulars of the issued share capital, loan capital, capital debt and any other significant liability of each of the Companies, together with the names and addresses of the persons in whose names such capital is registered or in whose favour such other liability has been incurred.

    (b) Whether any of those persons is acting as a nominee for some other person and, if so, the name and address of the beneficial owner.

    (c) Whether any person holds an option to purchase assets of, or an interest in, the Companies and, if so, a copy of the option agreement.

    (d) If any of the persons mentioned at (a), (b) or (c) above is a trustee or another company (other than one whose shares are quoted on a recognised stock exchange), a copy of the trust deed or (if a company) the names and addresses of the directors and also particulars as in (a), (b) and (c) above in respect of that other company.

4. Copies of the accounts of each of the Companies for all completed accounting periods since the dates of incorporation. Alternatively, if no accounts have been prepared in respect of these Companies, statements showing:

    (a) the assets and liabilities of each Company

        (i) as at the date of incorporation; and

        (ii) as at the date of the last completed accounting period,

    (b) all variations in those assets and liabilities (to include descriptions, dates of acquisition and disposal, and the full names and addresses of the persons from whom assets were acquired, other than by way of arm's length *bona fide* commercial transactions in the open market) between the date of incorporation and the date of the last completed accounting period,

(c) all income and expenditure (to include details of taxes paid) of each of the Companies during that period.

5. Particulars of any assets (including rights of any kind) transferred to or acquired by each of the Companies other than by way of an arm's-length transaction in the open market, showing in each case the name and address of the transferor or vendor and the consideration.

6. Copies of any contracts or agreements entered into by you at any time whereunder your services are to be (or were) provided to a person or persons resident or domiciled out of the United Kingdom.

7. Insofar as the information has not already been provided in your replies to paragraphs 3-6 above:

(a) Have you or your wife at any time been a settlor in relation to any settlement whatsoever?

(b) Subject to the exceptions below, have you or your wife at any time since   directly or indirectly made any transfer of assets to a person (or body of persons) at the time of the transfer or at any time subsequently resident outside the United Kingdom?

Exceptions

(i) Any transfer of assets not exceeding £ — in amount of value, unless the transfer formed part of a larger transaction or series of transactions whereby assets in excess of that amount or value were so transferred.

(ii) Any transfer of assets made solely in consideration for the supply of goods or services (other than services concerned with finance or investments) for the personal use of yourself or a member of your family.

(iii) Any transfer of assets made in the ordinary course of carrying on a trade or business provided that if this exception is relied on the trade or business shall be identified.

(iv) Any transfer of assets made in carrying out a purchase or sale of shares or securities through a recognised stock exchange.

(c) (i) Has any company (other than a quoted company), in which you or your wife now have or have at any time had any direct or indirect interest of any kind, made directly or indirectly at any time since any such transfer as in (b.) above (and subject to the same exceptions), being a transfer which you or your wife took any part in planning or bringing about or for which you or her consent, co-operation or approval was sought?

(ii) Have the trustees (or any one or more trustees) of a trust (or settlement) in which you or your wife now have at any time had any direct or indirect interest of any kind, made directly or indirectly at any time since any such transfer as in (b) above (and subject to the same exceptions), being a transfer which you or your wife took any part in planning or bringing about or for which your or her consent, co-operation or approval was sought?

(iii) Have the partners (or any one or more of the partners) of a partnership, in which you or your wife now have or at any time have had any direct or indirect interest of any kind, made directly or indirectly at any time since and such transfer as in (b) above (and subject to the same exceptions), being a transfer which you or your wife took any part in planning or bringing about or for which your or her consent, co-operation or approval was sought?

(iv) Has any person (or body of persons), in which or in the assets of which you or your wife now have or have at any time had any direct or indirect interest of any kind, made directly or indirectly at any time since any such transfer as in (b) above (and subject to the same exceptions), being a transfer which you or your wife took any part in planning or bringing about or for which your or her consent, co-operation or approval was sought and not being a transfer already disclosed in answer to paragraphs (i), (ii) or (iii) above?

(d) (i) Do you or your wife now have, or have you or your wife at any time since   had, any direct or indirect interest in any company which is or was at any time during which such interest subsisted resident outside the United Kingdom other than an interest which when first acquired was, and throughout the period during which it has been or was held by you or your wife has been or was, an interest in a quoted company or an interest held indirectly through a quoted company or a public unit trust?

(ii) Do you or your wife now have, or have you or your wife at any time since   had, any direct or indirect interest in any trust or settlement of which there is or was at any time during which such interest subsisted, a trustee resident outside the United Kingdom?

(iii) Do you or your wife now have, or have you or your wife at any time since   had, any direct or indirect interest in any partnership one or more partners of which is, or was at any time during which such interest subsisted, resident outside the United Kingdom?

(iv) Do your or your wife now have, or have you or your wife at any time since   had, any direct or indirect interest in any person (or body of persons) or the assets thereof which person (or body of persons) is or was at any time during which such interest subsisted resident outside the United Kingdom, not being an interest already disclosed in answer to paragraphs (i), (ii) or (iii) above?

(e) (i) Has any money or money's worth derived directly or indirectly from a company (other than a quoted company) at that time resident outside the United Kingdom been at any time since   paid to or put at the disposal of yourself or your wife or of a third party at your or her instance?

(ii) Has any money or money's worth derived directly or indirectly from a trust (or settlement) of which one or more trustees was at that time resident outside the United Kingdom been at any time since   paid to or put at the disposal of yourself or your wife or of a third party at your or her instance?

(iii) Has any money or money's worth derived directly or indirectly from a partnership of which one or more partners was at that time resident outside the United Kingdom been at any time since   paid to or put at the disposal of yourself or your wife or of a third party at your or her instance?

(iv) Has any money or money's worth not being money or money's worth disclosed in answer to paragraphs (i), (ii) or (iii) derived directly or indirectly from a person (or body of persons) or the assets thereof at a time when that person (or body of persons) was resident outside the United Kingdom been at any time since   paid to or put at the disposal of yourself or your wife or of a third party at your or her instance?

It is unnecessary to answer any paragraph of this question in respect of any money or money's worth which was income as distinct from capital in the hands of the recipient or which, unless it was a loan, was paid to or put at the disposal of yourself or your wife or of a third party at your or her instance by virtue of a transaction at arm's length.

8. If the answer to any of the questions in paragraph 7 above is in the affirmative, give full particulars in the case of Question (a) of each such settlement, in the case of each paragraph of Question (b) of each such transfer, in the case of each paragraph of Question (c) and (d) of each such interest, and in the case of each paragraph of Question (e) of all such money or money's worth. In all cases supply copies of any documents referred to in your answer and any documents by which any transaction referred to in your answer was wholly or partly carried out.

Dated

for the Commissioners of Inland Revenue

NOTICE UNDER SECTION 778 INCOME AND CORPORA-
TION TAXES ACT 1988

I,   , one of Her Majesty's Inspectors of Taxes, in exercise of my
powers under Section 778(1) of the Income and Corporation Taxes
Act 1988 hereby require you to furnish to me on or before   at
the address given above the particulars indicated in paragraph 3.
below.

2. INTERPRETATION

For the purpose of this notice:

(i) 'Persons' includes any company, partnership or firm.

(ii) 'Land' shall include buildings and any estate or interest in
land or buildings.

(iii) 'Interest in land' includes a future or contingent interest and
an option to acquire an interest; and the person shall be
treated as having an interest in land if the said land is held in
a settlement and if any benefit from the said settlement may
accrue to that person, directly or indirectly, through the
exercise of one or more powers or discretion.

(iv) 'Settlement' includes the definition given to this word in Section 681(4) Income and Corporation Taxes Act 1988.

(v) 'Relative' means a brother, sister, ancestor or lineal de-
scendant and includes

(a) a spouse or former spouse;

(b) any relative of yourself or your wife;

(c) the husband or wife of any relative of yourself, or of your
wife.

(vi) 'The specified transactions' shall mean

(A) The purchase on or around   by *A Ltd* of
land at

(B) The sale on or around   by *A Ltd* of land
at

(C) The purchase on or around   by *B Ltd* of
plots of land at

(D) The sale on or around   and   of
plots of land at

(E) etc to (O).

(P) Any purchase and/or sale of land by the above mentioned *A Ltd* and *B Ltd*, other than those transactions referred to at (A) to (O) above.

3. INFORMATION REQUIRED

In every case, where you have

(i)   been a party to a specified transaction or

(ii)   instructed or permitted any person or persons to act as your nominee or nominees or as your agent or agents, either directly or indirectly, in connection with a specified transaction.

You are hereby required to give the following particulars:

I.   full particulars of the specified transactions including the names and addresses of all parties concerned;

II.   the name and address of every person or persons introduced instructed or employed to act on behalf of any person in a specified transaction;

III.   the name and address of the person or persons for whom the benefit of a specified transaction arose or might arise and the nature of the benefit or possible benefit;

IV.   where any person named in the answer to III. above received, might have received or might receive directly or indirectly the said benefit and such person is an agent or nominee for some other person or persons, give the full name and address of such persons principal;

V.   where any party named in answer to I. above was acting for some other person or persons, the name and address of each such other person.

4. Without prejudice to the generality of paragraph 3. above, you are further required to give

(i)   in respect of each meeting with you attended or which was held by any company under your control, the date and place of the meeting, the names of the persons present, the capacity in which they attended and particulars of the discussion and decisions;

(ii)   in respect of each letter written or received by yourself or any company which you control, the names of the writer and addressee, the capacity in which each was concerned and particulars of the contents;

(iii)   in respect of each telephone conversation made either by yourself or on your behalf, the name of the other party, the capacity in which he was acting and full particulars of the contents;

(iv)   where any person named in the answer to any requirement in 3. and 4. above is a relative of yours, give the relationship.

Dated

H.M. Inspector of Taxes

APPENDIX 7. HANSARD EXTRACT AND QUESTIONS

Copy of answer given by the Chancellor of the Exchequer to a question asked in the House of Commons on 5 October 1944, regarding cases of fraud or wilful default in relation to Income Tax.

MAJOR STUDHOLME asked the Chancellor of the Exchequer what is the present practice of the Commissioners of Inland Revenue in regard to instituting criminal proceedings for alleged frauds on the Revenue.

SIR J. ANDERSON: The practice of the Commissioners in this matter is governed by Section 34 of the Finance Act 1942, which makes provision for the admissibility in evidence of any disclosure made in the circumstances there set out. As the Section indicates, the Commissioners have a general power under which they can accept pecuniary settlements instead of instituting criminal proceedings in respect of fraud or wilful default alleged to have been committed by a taxpayer. They can, however, give no undertaking to a taxpayer in any such case that they will accept such a settlement and refrain from instituting criminal proceedings even if the case is one in which the taxpayer has made full confession and has given full facilities for investigation of the facts. They reserve to themselves complete discretion in all cases as to the course which they will pursue, but it is their practice to be influenced by the fact that the taxpayer has made a full confession and has given full facilities for investigation into his affairs and for examination of such books, papers, documents or information as the Commissioners may consider necessary.

The above statement of the Commissioners' practice should be regarded as replacing the one made by my predecessor on the Second Reading of the Finance Bill 1942, which has, I understand, given rise to some misapprehension.

Section 34 of the Finance Act 1942 has been replaced successively by Section 504 of the Income Tax Act 1952 and (as from 6 April 1970) by Section 105 of the Taxes Management Act 1970. Section 105 reads as follows:

"105 – (1) Statements made or documents produced by or on behalf of a person shall not be inadmissible in any such proceedings as are mentioned in subsection (2) below by reason only that it has been drawn to his attention that:

(a) in relation to tax, the Board may accept pecuniary settlements instead of instituting proceedings, and

(b) though no undertaking can be given as to whether or not the Board will accept such a settlement in the case of any particular person, it is the practice of the Board to be influenced by the fact that a person has made a full confession of any fraud or default to which he has been a party, and has given full facilities for investigation, and that he was or may have been induced thereby to make the statements or produce the documents.

(2) The proceedings mentioned in subsection (1) above are:

(a) any criminal proceedings against the person in question for any form of fraud or wilful default in connection with or in relation to tax, and

(b) any proceedings against him for the recovery of any sum due from him, whether by way of tax or penalty, in connection with or in relation to tax."

In the 1970 Act, "the Board" means the Commissioners of Inland Revenue, and "tax", where neither income tax nor capital gains tax nor corporation tax is specified, means any of those taxes (see Section 118 (1)). Section 34 of the Finance Act 1942 was extended to the profits tax and excess profits tax by Section 28 (2) of the Finance Act 1943; and Section 504 of the Income Tax Act 1952 was applied to excess profits levy by Section 64 (3) of the Finance Act 1952.

Hansard Questions

i.   In regard to any business with which you or your wife have been concerned either as director, partner or sole proprietor,

    a. have any transactions, receipts or expenses been omitted from or incorrectly recorded in the books thereof?

    b. are the accounts sent to the Inland Revenue correct and complete to the best of your knowledge and belief?

    c. are taxation returns correct and complete to the best of your knowledge and belief?

ii. Are all your personal taxation returns correct and complete to the best of your knowledge and belief?

iii. Are you prepared to allow examination of all business books, business and private bank statements and other business and private records in order that the Revenue may be satisfied that your answers to the first two questions are correct?

		JAN	FEB	MAR	APR
Table of interest factors as at 1st of month	1965	.840	.8425	.845	.8475
	1966	.870	.8725	.875	.8775
(To use the table	1967	.900	.9025	.905	.9075
subtract the normal due date for payment (see	1968	.9367	.940	.9433	.9467
pages 47 and 90) from the expected date of payment	1969	.9767	.980	.9833	.9867
and multiply out the tax due on the difference)	1970	1.0167	1.020	1.0233	1.0267
	1971	1.0567	1.060	1.0633	1.0667
	1972	1.0967	1.100	1.1033	1.1067
	1973	1.1367	1.140	1.1433	1.1467
	1974	1.1767	1.180	1.1833	1.1867
	1975	1.242	1.2495	1.257	1.2645
	1976	1.332	1.3395	1.347	1.3545
	1977	1.422	1.4295	1.437	1.4445
	1978	1.512	1.5195	1.527	1.5345
	1979	1.602	1.6095	1.617	1.6245
	1980	1.692	1.702	1.712	1.722
	1981	1.812	1.822	1.832	1.842
	1982	1.932	1.942	1.952	1.962
	1983	2.0487	2.0553	2.062	2.0687
	1984	2.1287	2.1353	2.142	2.1487
	1985	2.2087	2.2153	2.222	2.2287
	1986	2.3087	2.3178	2.3270	2.3362
	1987	2.4098	2.4178	2.4257	2.4336
	1988	2.4987	2.5056	2.5125	2.5193

MAY	JUN	JUL	AUG	SEPT	OCT	NOV	DEC
.850	.8525	.855	.8575	.860	.8625	.865	.8675
.880	.8825	.885	.8875	.890	.8925	.895	.8975
.910	.9133	.9167	.920	.9233	.9267	.930	.9333
.950	.9533	.9567	.960	.9633	.9667	.970	.9733
.990	.9933	.9967	1.000	1.0033	1.0067	1.010	1.0133
1.030	1.0333	1.0367	1.040	1.0433	1.0467	1.050	1.0533
1.070	1.0733	1.0767	1.080	1.0833	1.0867	1.090	1.0933
1.110	1.1133	1.1167	1.120	1.1233	1.1267	1.130	1.1333
1.150	1.1533	1.1567	1.160	1.1633	1.1667	1.170	1.1733
1.190	1.1933	1.197	1.2045	1.212	1.2195	1.227	1.2345
1.272	1.2795	1.287	1.2945	1.302	1.3095	1.317	1.3245
1.362	1.3695	1.377	1.3845	1.392	1.3995	1.407	1.4145
1.452	1.4595	1.467	1.4745	1.482	1.4895	1.497	1.5015
1.542	1.5495	1.557	1.5645	1.572	1.5795	1.587	1.5945
1.632	1.6395	1.647	1.6545	1.662	1.6695	1.677	1.6845
1.732	1.742	1.752	1.762	1.772	1.782	1.792	1.802
1.852	1.862	1.872	1.882	1.892	1.902	1.912	1.922
1.972	1.982	1.992	2.002	2.012	2.022	2.032	2.042
2.0753	2.082	2.0887	2.0953	2.102	2.1087	2.1153	2.122
2.1553	2.162	2.1687	2.1753	2.182	2.1887	2.1953	2.202
2.2353	2.2445	2.2537	2.2628	2.2720	2.2812	2.2903	2.2995
2.3453	2.3545	2.3637	2.3728	2.3799	2.3870	2.3940	2.4019
2.4411	2.4486	2.4555	2.4624	2.4693	2.4768	2.4843	2.4918
2.5262	2.5327	2.5391	2.5456	2.5520	2.5585	2.5649	2.5714

APPENDIX 8

Normal due dates to use for Section 88 Interest

Tax	*Nature of Income*	*Due date for S.88 Interest*
Income tax Schedule A	Income from property	1 January of year of assessment.
Income tax Schedule D	Income from trades, professions, vocations Untaxed interest Foreign income Annual profits not chargeable under other Schedules	1 January of year of assessment, unless payable in two instalments, in which case 1 April of year of assessment.
Income tax Schedule E	Income from office or employment	1 January of year of assessment.
Capital gains tax	Capital gains	Up to 1979/80 6 July following year of assessment. Thereafter 1 December following year of assessment.
Corporation tax	Company profits	Nine months from end of chargeable accounting period.
Section 286 tax	Loans/advances to directors/shareholders	1st day of financial year following that in which loan or advance is made.

APPENDIX 9. PENALTY ABATEMENTS

EXTRACT FROM INLAND REVENUE GUIDANCE LEAFLET (IR 73)

The penalty figure will normally be a percentage of the tax underpaid or paid late. In strict law it could be more than 100% of the amount of tax or even, in cases of fraud, more than 200%. In practice it is always less than that. The Inspector never seeks a penalty of more than 100% of the tax. That figure is further reduced by an amount which depends upon whether you disclosed all the details of your tax affairs, the extent to which you co-operated in the enquiry and the gravity of the offence.

The reductions are as follows:

Disclosure – a reduction of up to 20% (or even 30% for voluntary disclosure).

If you have made a full and voluntary disclosure before the Inspector challenges you, you will get a considerable reduction of the penalty. If you deny until the last possible moment that there is anything wrong, you will not get any reduction for disclosure at all.

Between these two extremes a wide variety of circumstances is possible. The Inspector has to consider how much information you gave, how soon, and how that contributed towards settling the investigation.

Co-operation – a reduction of up to 40%

You can supply information promptly, attend interviews, answer questions honestly and accurately, give all the relevant facts and pay tax on account when it becomes possible to estimate the amount due. You will then get the maximum reduction for co-operation.

You will get none at all if you put off supplying information, avoid attending interviews, give untrue answers to questions, do nothing until formal proceedings are taken against you and generally obstruct the course of the investigation.

Between these extremes there is a wide range of possible circumstances and the Inspector has to compare the extent you have co-operated with the co-operation he or she believes possible.

Gravity – a reduction of up to 40%

Your actions may amount to a premeditated and well organised fraud or something much less serious. The Inspector has to take into account what you did, how you did it, how long it went on and the

93

amounts of money involved. The less serious your offence, the bigger
the reduction of penalty will be.

DELOITTE HASKINS & SELLS
OFFICES IN THE BRITISH ISLES

Aberdeen
6 Golden Square,
Aberdeen AB9 1JB.
Telephone: (0224) 636555

Belfast
Northern Bank House,
10 High Street,
Belfast BT1 2BL.
Telephone: (0232) 246969

Birmingham
35 Newhall Street,
Birmingham B3 3DX.
Telephone: 021-200 2828

Bristol
Bull Wharf,
Redcliff Street,
Bristol BS99 7TR.
Telephone: (0272) 260514

Cambridge
Mount Pleasant House,
Huntingdon Road,
Cambridge CB3 0BL.
Telephone: (0223) 314992

Cardiff
Tudor House, 16 Cathedral Road,
Cardiff CF1 6PN.
Telephone: (0222) 239944

Croydon
Melrose House,
42 Dingwall Road,
Croydon CR0 2NE.
Telephone: 01-681 5252

Edinburgh
P.O. Box 90,
25 Abercromby Place,
Edinburgh EH3 6QS.
Telephone: 031-557 3333

Glasgow
100 Wellington Street,
Glasgow G2 6DJ.
Telephone: 041-248 7932

Gloucester
Lennox House,
Beaufort Buildings,
Spa Road, Gloucester GL1 1XD.
Telephone: (0452) 423031

Leeds
Cloth Hall Court, Infirmary Street,
Leeds LS1 2HT.
Telephone: (0532) 455166

Liverpool
Richmond House,
1 Rumford Place,
Liverpool L3 2HT.
Telephone: 051-227 4242

London
P.O. Box 207,
128 Queen Victoria Street,
London EC4P 4JX.
Telephone: 01-248 3913

P.O. Box 198
Hillgate House,
26 Old Bailey,
London EC4M 7PL.
Telephone: 01-248 3913

Manchester
Bank House,
Charlotte Street,
Manchester M1 4BX.
Telephone: 061-236 9565

Newcastle upon Tyne
Hadrian House, Higham Place,
Newcastle upon Tyne NE1 8BP.
Telephone: 091-261 2121

Norwich
7 Queen Street,
Norwich NR2 4ST.
Telephone: (0603) 624181

Nottingham
Compass House,
The Ropewalk,
Nottingham NG1 5DQ.
Telephone: (0602) 419066

Reading
P.O. Box 147,
Venture House,
37/43 Blagrave Street,
Reading RG1 1RY.
Telephone: (0734) 596711

Southampton
Wheatsheaf House,
24 Bernard Street,
Southampton SO9 1QL.
Telephone: (0703) 634521

Swansea
P.O. Box 60,
Midland Bank Chambers,
Castle Square,
Swansea SA1 1DU.
Telephone: (0792) 475777

Channel Islands
Whiteley Chambers,
Don Street,
St. Helier, Jersey, C.I.
Telephone: (0534) 75151

Town Mills, South, Rue du Pré
St. Peter Port, Guernsey, C.I.
Telephone: (0481) 728278

Republic of Ireland
43-49 Mespil Road,
Dublin 4.
Telephone: (0001) 604400/605500

European Communities Office
Avenue de Cortenberg 79/81,
Boite 7, B1040, Brussels.
Telephone: 02 736 2058

Energy Choices

Edited by Christina Hughes

Series Editor: Cara Acred

Vol.100

Independence Educational Publishers

First published by Independence

The Studio, High Green, Great Shelford

Cambridge CB22 5EG

England

© Independence 2015

Copyright

This book is sold subject to the condition that it shall not, by way of trade or otherwise, be lent, resold, hired out or otherwise circulated in any form of binding or cover other than that in which it is published without the publisher's prior consent.

Photocopy licence

The material in this book is protected by copyright. However, the purchaser is free to make multiple copies of particular articles for instructional purposes for immediate use within the purchasing institution. Making copies of the entire book is not permitted.

British Library Cataloguing in Publication Data

Energy choices. -- (Issues today ; 100)

1. Power resources--Juvenile literature.

I. Series II. Acred, Cara editor.

333.7'9-dc23

ISBN-13: 9781861687159

ROTHERHAM SCHOOLS LOANS SERVICE	
55 028 433 4	
CPA213624	J333.79
PETERS	£5.95

Acknowledgements

The publisher is grateful for permission to reproduce the material in this book. While every care has been taken to trace and acknowledge copyright, the publisher tenders its apology for any accidental infringement or where copyright has proved untraceable. The publisher would be pleased to come to a suitable arrangement in any such case with the rightful owner.

Illustrations

All illustrations, including the front cover, are by Don Hatcher, except for page 23 by Simon Kneebone.

Images

Page 1: Openclipart.org, page 6: Icons from Freepik, page 7: MorgueFile, page 11: Icons from Freepik, page 13: MorgueFile, page 14: Icons from Freepik, page 16: iStock, page 20: MorgueFile, page 22: MorgueFile, page 24: Icons from Freepik and page 25: © Intel Free Press.

Editorial by Christina Hughes and layout by Jackie Staines, on behalf of Independence Educational Publishers.

Printed in Great Britain by Zenith Print Group.

Cara Acred

Cambridge

May 2015